IGNITE
YOUR CULTURE

6 Steps to Fuel
Your People, Profits
and Potential

IGNITE
YOUR CULTURE

**6 Steps to Fuel
Your People, Profits
and Potential**

Carol Ring

Ignite Your Culture:
6 Steps to Fuel Your People, Profits and Potential

By Carol Ring

Copyright © 2014 by Carol Ring

Published by Figment Publishing

www.carolring.ca

Production Management by Janet Spencer King

www.bookdevelopmentgroup.com

janet.sp.king@verizon.net

Cover design and interior design by LMW Design Inc.

www.lmwdesign.com

To contact the author or to order additional copies of this book, e-mail: carol@carolring.ca

Printed in Canada

For worldwide distribution

ISBN 978-0-9921004-1-4

You get the best effort from others
not by lighting a fire beneath them,
but by building a fire within.

—Bob Nelson

Table of Contents

Introduction

The values and beliefs of leaders drive the culture of an organization. And the culture of an organization fuels its potential. With an understanding of culture, along with proven assessment tools and processes, leaders can ignite a culture that allows employees, and the organization, to grow into their full potential.

Leaders have spent too much time focusing on the physical assets of their companies. Yes, as a leader, you've probably become more enlightened about employee relations over the past two decades and upped your company's internal communications, performance-management systems, and hiring practices. It's time to acknowledge today's organizations are not about products, slogans, and manufacturing lines. *They're all about the people.* People, not products, produce profits. When people gather together in a workplace, an organizational culture is born.

What could any of this "culture" talk have to do with creating shareholder value and improving bottom-line results? And yet, culture has become a critical component in business success, and you'll soon see why the concept goes beyond the cliché "Happy employees make happy customers."

In my career, I've worked with happy employees, and I've

spent lots of time being a disillusioned, frustrated employee. I've enjoyed the excitement of achievement and the relief of getting past an ugly phase. These are turning points you may relate to as well. Like me, you've probably shared stories with family, at cocktail parties, and on leadership panels. These stories reflect our greatest business successes and our biggest challenges.

Often, a common theme emerges in describing these storied situations—and it's rarely about the product. Rather, it's about the terrible boss or the customer from hell. It's about the sales clerk with "attitude" or the co-worker who drives you crazy. Every now and again, it's about the people you enjoy working with and the leaders you hold in deep respect. One way or another, it's about *people*.

I remember the days when leaders motivated employees by reminding them that, without a product or customers, there would be no revenue and therefore no paychecks and no business. It's time to displace products and customers from the top of the paradigm and place a higher priority on our own people. In fact, it's not accurate to say "move people to the top of the priority list"; it's their *values* that should top that list. Values and beliefs create the culture of all companies.

Intuitively, the goal is to build a workplace in which employees want to come to work and others want to apply. So as leaders, we follow the trends on flex time, improved benefits, and employee surveys. However, we also deal in a world of shareholder value, key business indicators, and strategy maps. Fitting "happy employees" into this structure is complicated, so why bother? Embarking on an exercise to improve culture is seen by many as being costly. For others it's just not a priority, and quite possibly it's just a passing business fad.

And yet, organizations that create a strong positive culture are more successful than those that don't. They use culture as a competitive advantage. When culture is aligned with branding, customer loyalty is stronger. In times of crisis, a strong culture is resilient. And in a world of ever-increasing numbers of mergers and acquisitions a focus on culture can maximize the synergies and benefits of these activities.

During my 25 years in industry I have experienced the good and bad when it comes to culture. I've come to understand the impact of leaders on the culture of the workplace. It doesn't matter if you're at the top of a large multinational corporation or the manager of a single department. The values of the leaders influence the culture. If you're a leader who values innovation, that's the tone you'll set.

When I worked in an environment of positive culture, the tasks were interesting and the time flew by. There was a sense of pride and teamwork. One of the best companies I ever worked for was a franchise bottler of Coca-Cola. And that's not just be-cause of the Coca-Cola product. It's because the President, David Dick, was such an amazing leader. It was early in my career, but I've never forgotten how enjoyable the work was. Yes there were challenges, like in any organization, however Mr. Dick ran the company with integrity, providing support and recognition to every employee. He was all about growing the business—and indeed, his focus on his people drove a profitable business.

There have also been times when my work environment

was not so rosy. Those were tough days to get out of bed and motivate myself to drive to the office. Times were tough economically, infighting over scarce resources was prevalent, and leadership was lacking. It wasn't so clear at the beginning, but it became clear later on how the behaviors of the leaders influenced the culture, the office atmosphere, and employee productivity.

I've studied and used Cultural Assessment Tools that have proved to me that culture is more than touchy-feely sentiment. It is possible to measure culture and it's also possible to measure the degree of energy being spent on unproductive work as a result of poor culture. For me, at first, creating a great culture was more about moving intuitively away from the things that were barriers to my employees' productivity. Things like bureaucracy, lack of teamwork, and poor communications. However, once I became aware of tangible tools available to measure culture, it became easy to define the starting point and the direction to take to improve the culture. And as it improved, people were happier, more productive, and more focused on the tasks at hand.

I've also developed a process to successfully move a culture from one by default to one by design. In this book we will discuss how culture does play with profits, how a culture evolves with its leader, and how to IGNITE your existing culture. IGNITE is a process that will teach you about using the right culture assessment tools to **I**nquire and **G**ather information about your current and desired culture. You'll see how critical it is to **N**ame and define the values required to move your organization forward. The next step will show you how to **I**mbed people, processes and policies into the strategies and day-to-day operations of your business that will move your culture from where it is today to where it needs to be. Building the right reports to **T**rack your culture initiatives and keep them top of mind is key to creating action and culture change. As you move through your culture shift, it's important to check in and **E**valuate if your culture is shifting or not as a result of the initiatives you're putting in place.

Every chapter contains a small exercise at the end to help you connect the topic to your own current situation. I've called them Fuel for Thought, because every fire needs kindling wood to get things started. Take the time to reflect on these questions, jot down some of your observations, and use them later as inspiration to move forward.

John Quincy Adams once said "If your actions inspire others to dream more, learn more, do more and become more, you are a leader." I want you to embrace the culture in your organization because I've seen firsthand the impact of strong positive cultures. Culture is the fuel within an organization. Not only does it fuel results, it fuels people. Achievements are wonderful, but potential is even better. I believe the greatest role a leader can play is to provide the right environment for people and organizations to develop and grow into their potential.

But even good leaders need help to know what actions to take. I've spent years researching, testing and working through the activities required to bring about strong positive cultures. This book is about actions, concrete steps you can take to better understand the impact of culture and how to ignite the culture in your organization. In the words of Walt Disney *"The way to get started is to quit talking and begin doing."* That's why this book is for you!

CHAPTER ONE:

Culture's Influence on Corporate Results

Management guru Peter Drucker once said, "Culture eats strategy for breakfast."

How can this be so? When a company's strategic hand contains such high cards as mission, vision, and objectives, how can company culture be the trump card? After all, a well-thought plan to achieve the organization's overarching financial goals will carry a company forward without the ideal environment for employees. And in fact, many companies have flourished without understanding *anything* about corporate culture. Yet all leaders set the tone for a corporate culture within their organizations, whether or not they understand that culture or know it exists. So how does corporate culture affect strategy?

Consider this example. The leaders of a large energy company with divisions across two regions decided to implement a new dispatch system for their field technicians. Frank, the chief operating officer, was assigned to be the overall executive sponsor for the project. To lead the project, the company brought in an experienced external consultant who assembled a team with representatives from the two regions. Frank met with team members quarterly to remind them about the importance of the project to the company. He would diligently go around the room thanking participants for doing their best to keep team members motivated and engaged. The team established well-defined objectives that included streamlining processes, reducing costs, and improving productivity. Moving to one new system meant both teams had to agree on how that system would approach workforce management. The teams also participated in the testing process and became familiar with the system before it went live.

They first implemented the new system with a small division in the eastern region. Unfortunately, problems appeared that had not been raised during testing. For the first time, local management had real-time access to their technicians' activities. Dispatchers now flagged issues such as late starts and non-compliance on their computer screens. Technicians became upset, feeling that the dispatchers were trying to define their workday, whereas before, they had felt empowered to create their own routes.

In keeping with a small "test" implementation, the project team logged these new issues, developed fixes, enhanced the system, and sent memos reminding employees of the new processes. The rollout continued until both regions were fully operational on the new system.

However, problems continued in the eastern region. Instead of reducing the company's costs, the region's management brought in additional resources to manage the issues. The western region, on the other hand, achieved the project objectives of increasing productivity and reducing costs. What made the difference? Feedback showed the western region had focused on new tools to help technicians better serve the customers.

Week after week, the executive sponsor listened while the eastern region's leadership team related their explanations. Exasperated, the executive sponsor finally called the two regional heads together. He had to find out how implementing the same system, developed by a combined working team, could have resulted in two such different outcomes. In their meeting, the two regional heads agreed the objectives had been clear. Representatives from both regions had defined the requirements for the new system and participated in the same training program. So what went wrong?

Remember Frank's visits with the working team, declaring the project a key imperative for the corporation? Unfortunately, his diligence didn't extend to the eastern regional head who, instead of participating in the implementation, took that week off to vacation in Paris. By contrast, the western regional head had been onsite during the conversion weekend and made himself visible to his dispatch team during the first two weeks. It's no wonder that when Frank visited the two dispatch centers to hear from the employees themselves, the stories he heard were as different as day and night.

Specifically, the eastern region employees were frustrated, highlighting all kinds of faults in the system. In contrast, the western region employees were more forward thinking. They described ways they could use the new system to generate even more benefits than those achieved to date.

Even though the company followed all the right steps to

develop the same strategy for both regions, culture won out in the end. Let's look at additional differences between the corporate cultures in each region.

Clearly, the eastern region had developed a culture of blame, buck-passing, and risk-averse behavior. The dispatchers blamed the IT folks and complained about the operations manager's inability to get the technicians on the road on time. The operations manager complained that the dispatcher manager didn't have enough resources and technicians were standing around with no work. The technicians blamed the dispatchers. None of them were interested in hearing about the new system. The region's corporate culture was broken.

By contrast, the western region had a culture of accountability, teamwork, customer service, and innovation. The employees knew the limitations of the old system and were excited to try a more user-friendly one. They welcomed an automated system that took over the assignment of daily routing and work instead of leaving that to the discretion of the dispatchers and technicians. After all, no one could complain that the IT system was playing favorites. Instead of focusing on entitlement, the western region technicians wanted to help as many customers as possible in a day. With that goal in mind, they couldn't wait to start their day on time.

Because upper management failed to recognize the regional differences in culture, they hugely underestimated the change required to implement the new system for the eastern region. They weren't prepared to manage that amount of change—and even if they had been, the eastern region's culture wouldn't have allowed for sustainable change. In retrospect, management had to address the region's foundation—its culture—first. By not addressing the culture, the cost of the IT implementation was much higher than planned. Just imagine how this poor culture was impacting other parts of the business, driving even more costs into the operations.

The Role Values Play

Many studies have shown a link between corporate performance and organizations that practice a values-driven, culturally aware approach. In one study, a U.S. hospital addressed its cultural issues and succeeded in reducing staff turnover from 24 percent to 15 percent. In another, an Australian Bank re-focused on culture and moved employee satisfaction from 49 percent to 85 percent over five years. And in a third study, an African engineering company changed its culture and boosted its headline earnings from 300 million to 2.2 billion rand!

Kotter and Heskett of Harvard Business School carried out a four-year study of culture in nine to 10 firms from each of 20 industries. They found that firms with a strong adaptive culture based on shared values outperformed firms with rigid or weak cultures by a significant margin. In the companies with a healthy culture, revenue grew more than four times faster, the rate of job creation was seven times higher, stock grew 12 times faster, and profits were 750 times higher! According to Great Place to Work research, done over a 15-year period from 1997 to 2012, Fortune's Best Companies to Work For provided three times the cumulative stock market return over the S&P 500.

They also generated 10.8% annualized stock market returns compared to less than 5% for the S&P 500. The business case is clear: Strong positive cultures are returning strong bottom lines.

The competitive environment is shifting. It's not enough anymore to create a strategy. It's not enough to build out the tactics to implement your strategy's initiatives. It's not even enough to institutionalize good change-management practices. All of that work goes for naught if you don't address the core foundation of your company—its corporate culture.

It's called "corporate culture capital"—the next leading advantage for boosting your company's performance.

FUEL FOR THOUGHT

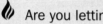 Are you letting culture "eat" your strategy?

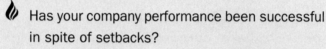 Has your company performance been successful in spite of setbacks?

How will you embrace the cultural capital frontier and deal yourself the best possible hand?

CHAPTER TWO

How Leaders Fuel Culture

"Corporate Culture, Corporate Smulture, who really needs it anyway? Bottom-line results are all that count in my business."

Many leaders may still think this way when they're struggling to get through yet another tough quarter and their company's physical assets are a more immediate concern than its human assets. Other leaders agree a company needs to look after its employees, so they say something like, "Let's run an employee engagement survey. And just to go one better, let's develop some corporate values we can rally the troops behind."

Sounds like a good start, right? Let's look at a hypothetical example of how this process might play out in practice.

Upper-level managers at Outrageously Average Inc. have heard that satisfied employees generate satisfied customers, so they decide to make changes to increase employee motivation. The company's accountants have pointed out the cost of employee turnover. That tells top managers that employee retention is important to control this cost. They even understand that culture has an impact on the company's bottom line.

So the managers venture outside their comfort zones and

decide to measure the company's current corporate values. They bring in experts with cultural measurement tools, such as Cultural Values Assessments and Cultural Entropy Reports. They convene the senior leadership team around a table to discuss the ideal values for the company. All the right buzzwords make their way onto the list: teamwork, fun, innovation, trust, integrity, customer focus.

The managers then survey employees about the values *they'd* like to see in the company. Many of the same words show up. "Well, that's good news," the managers think. "They want what we want!"

Armed with a list of buzzwords, management organizes an employee forum and rallies the troops. They hand out laminated cards and hang "Successories" motivational posters to remind people about these *highly important values.*

After a year or so, the company conducts a follow-up survey to see how the shift toward a new culture is coming along. Unfortunately, not much seems to have changed. Instead of the positive values everyone agreed to, the managers hear complaints about bureaucracy, blame, information hoarding, and "silos"—isolation of each department from the rest. Puzzled, they ask, "Why don't our employees get it? Why isn't the change happening?"

But like many leaders, Outrageously Average Inc.'s managers fail to understand that a current culture survey actually measures the *behaviors and beliefs of management.* They believe the company's culture reflects the values of all its employees. In fact, employees have observed the leadership team's behaviors, and they've noticed the leaders are still asking for several levels of sign-offs and approvals. It appears to the employees the leaders don't trust them so they've kept all the bureaucracy in place. Managers are still blaming each other, and no one challenges them to stop behaving this way. If the leaders won't change their behaviors, then why should the rest of the employees? And if the bureaucratic processes and policies won't be addressed by the leadership team, then how will bureaucracy ever disappear?

Albert Schweitzer once said, "Example is not the main thing in influencing others, it is the only thing." Research has demonstrated this phenomenon over and over, with a high correlation between current culture assessments and values assessments of the leaders. Doing a corporate current values assessment is much like conducting a 360-degree review for your leaders. If a leader consistently demonstrates teamwork and creates the right conditions for teamwork, then teamwork will likely show up in a current values assessment. If a leader doesn't take accountability and constantly blames others, then there's a good chance that blame will show up in the current values assessment. Clearly, leaders set the tone for others to follow.

At every level of the organization, a values assessment is likely to mirror the behaviors and beliefs of the person in charge. And when leaders stress the importance of certain values but act in a manner that doesn't support those values, they confuse their employees.

A Leader's Style Always Influences Others

You may have experienced the "command and control" leader who directs and micro-manages but doesn't lead by example. Or perhaps you've had the good fortune to work under transformational leaders. These leaders have a strong vision of where they want to take the company. They engage, collaborate, and develop their employees to grow the organization. Either way, it's a good bet that each of your bosses' behaviors and belief systems influenced the culture for their company, division, or unit.

For example, I worked at one of Canada's largest telecommunications companies, Rogers Communications, for 24 years. Over this time span, I witnessed the company's tremendous growth from a small entrepreneurial cable business to a hugely expanded Internet and wireless communications company. In the process, I worked for many different CEOs, including the company's founder Ted Rogers. Each leader brought his or her unique style, values, and purpose.

Rogers, as the title of his recent biographical book suggests, was "relentless" in his desire for innovation, growth, and challenging the status quo. Creating Canada's largest telecommunications company meant everything to him. He valued this vision so strongly, he virtually worked a 24/7 week, and he expected his employees to value this same work ethic. For him, successful employees also had to value risk-taking and constant change. Risk-averse people who favored a slow, stable environment were likely to find working at Rogers difficult.

At the same time, the company's ambitious pace during some of those early years meant that Ted focused on innovation over employee motivation. Not to say he didn't offer his thanks for a job well done; he did so often. However, celebrations of success were fleeting. It was always time to move on to the next great initiative.

In one case I recall, I worked on a complex real estate plan for our operations in eastern Ontario. I had worked diligently to put together a detailed plan and recommendation. I assumed Ted would read it within 24 hours and return it to me with his comments. From experience, I also knew my draft plan wouldn't be the final version, but I looked forward to taking a break from the project, even for a short 24 hours. That's why I purposely didn't fax the report to our Toronto office until almost 6 p.m., figuring Ted would have packed up his work by then and left the office. I thought that would guarantee my report wouldn't be in his overnight pile, and he wouldn't see it until the next day—giving me that welcome one-day reprieve.

Not so! I arrived at the office the next morning with great anticipation to start work on something new and fresh. But there on my desk, I found a return fax with Ted's thanks, his comments scratched throughout the document, and of course, his request for immediate turnaround on the next draft.

Ted always communicated a sense of urgency—and that urgency created the change and momentum he deemed so important to the company's growth and success. He modeled a culture that expected employees to work hard, take only a brief moment to embrace progress, and then get on with a project's next phase.

Rogers CEO Jos Wintermans was much more deliberate than Ted Rogers—and no less visionary. But by contrast, Jos was all about people. He conducted a full analysis of the organizational structure of the company, which was incredibly complex at the time. Attempting to depict the organization pictorially, he pasted sheets of brown paper on the walls of a large boardroom. And while his chart showed lots of boxes connected by lines indicating multiple reporting relationships, I noticed three boxes with no lines. The three people whose names appeared in those boxes didn't know whom they reported to, and no department leaders had claimed them on the charts they'd provided.

In addition, when asked to provide the job descriptions of each employee, managers observed duplicate accountabilities. Finally, they identified areas where significant work had fallen through the cracks as employees simply pushed papers from one level of the organization to another. Clearly, we'd succeeded to this point *in spite of* poor organization!

From there, Jos developed a vision and process to demystify our complex organizational structure and create meaningful work for everyone. But he also had little tolerance for those who didn't share the same corporate values. Employees who weren't able to conform to the new behaviors found themselves outside the renewed organization. If an employee was confused about the shift but willing to adjust, Jos provided constructive advice about how he expected employees to demonstrate the new values. Teamwork was key; it was no longer acceptable to declare success just because you knew how to maneuver the complex organization and manage others in a "command and control" manner.

To achieve a new organization chart that made sense, every vice president in the company (about 65 people) spent days locked in a large hotel ballroom moving from one functional group to another, sorting out the lines of accountability between the groups. Thanks to the new focus and value placed on the human assets of the company, we emerged at the end of the organizational design exercise with an energized and focused workforce. We spent many months afterward formalizing the new leadership team, new organizational structure, and new way of working together. No more unclaimed, isolated boxes floated among the lines of the organization charts.

In short, Ted Rogers and Jos Wintermans had different management styles, and one wasn't objectively better than the other. However, those two styles resulted from each leader's personal values, beliefs, and behaviors. Both styles affected the company's culture.

Every leader has his or her own beliefs and values, which translate into behaviors. It's these behaviors that define the current culture. When receiving a current culture assessment from their employees, they must be prepared to acknowledge the role they've played in creating the current environment. And sometimes that assessment won't paint as rosy a picture as what they expect. It's never a pleasant thing to receive the results of a negative current culture assessment. Most leaders probably react with denial, anger, or even depression before they accept difficult feedback. They might think, "The survey must be flawed."

Or "the right people weren't included in the survey. Are you sure you didn't mix up my results with one of our other divisions?" Or "What kind of experts are these consultants anyway; don't we know our people better than anyone?"

But at the end of the day, leaders must be accountable for the results—whatever the results are! It's only with the leaders' personal transformation that a true organizational shift can take place. As business thought leader Tom Peters said, "The role of the leader is to manage the values of the corporation." And this includes the leaders' own values and behaviors.

That doesn't mean you need to hire a whole new leadership team to correct culture; that's an extreme solution. After all, leaders come with all kinds of expertise the business needs. Sometimes, increased self-awareness about how they come across to employees is enough to help them make small shifts that ripple throughout the organization. Executive coaching can be used effectively to identify root causes behind a leader's behaviors. Then the coach provides exercises and support to adjust those behaviors and activate the desired values within those on the leadership team.

Missing a Big Competitive Edge

If you don't take into account the impact leaders have on corporate culture, you're missing a big competitive edge. Cultivating leaders with the right expertise *and* the right behaviors are key to taking any business to the next level.

Imagine you have two organizations with the same "average" culture in which employee satisfaction meets or just exceeds the industry norms. However, only one organization recognizes the impact of their leadership team on that culture. Over time, these aware leaders work together on their values and behaviors and elevate the company from an "average" culture of short-term focus, profit, and customer satisfaction to one of continuous improvement, financial stability, and making a difference. Employees in this transformed organization are not only satisfied to come to work every day; they are overwhelmingly enthusiastic about it. Imagine the uplift in productivity and decline in employee turnover. This organization will end up in an enviable competitive position.

Now, let's be clear. There's more to transforming a corporate culture than simply shifting the behaviors of the leaders. If you have a bureaucratic culture and want to move to one of empowerment, not only do the leaders need to model and encourage empowerment, they also need to update the company's processes and policies to complement the desired change. But to think transformation can happen without addressing the values and behaviors of the leadership team is naïve. It all starts with the leaders, period.

FUEL FOR THOUGHT

❦ What are you as leaders in your organization doing to contribute to your corporate culture?

❦ How much of your corporate culture is a direct result of the personal values of your leadership team?

❦ How honest are you being about your role in the creation of your division's culture?

CHAPTER THREE

How Employees Fuel Culture

The strategic planning cycle for your company is about to begin again. It's time to check in on your mission, vision, and values, as well as the strategies you've outlined to move the organization forward.

You've gathered your balanced scorecard, your employee satisfaction surveys, and the external competitive landscape. You and your executive team have worked hard over the past two years to take the corporate strategies and roll them down throughout the organization, aligning key goals of leadership with those of employees.

You've held town hall meetings and team barbeques to ensure your employees are clear on the company's direction. You've clarified the desired values and updated your performance management system to include demonstrating these key values. You've pulled out the company's previous tactical plans and rated the progress. You've done some process re-engineering and reorganized the corporate structure.

Yet the company's financial performance hasn't improved as expected. Your employee satisfaction results are slipping. Your competition is getting stronger, putting even more pressure on you. You so carefully laid out and assembled the intricate recipe for success, but you feel as if you've ended up with a bland dish. You sit with your team in confusion. What went wrong? What's the secret ingredient that's missing from this corporate sauce?

The answer: The strategy to implement your plan didn't have any reference or attention to culture. That's why you often find yourself with binders of ideas to improve the organization but can't lift the ideas off the paper. If the idea involves innovation and yet the culture values the status quo, you'll encounter immense resistance to shifting to innovation. You can't create innovation just by putting the right words on a wall or in a strategic plan. You have to *cultivate* a culture of innovation.

For an example, let's look again at Frank, the energy company CEO in Chapter 1. He's responsible for the company's operations. Each unit within his scope handles hundreds of orders every day. Customer orders pass from the sales team to the warehouse to the dispatch team to the installer, and then back to the billing team. All the work is tightly linked, and the strength of the chain is based on the weakest link.

To review this work flow and the dependencies between each phase of the order flow, Frank brought in a team of "process re-engineering" experts. The team reviewed the process flow and identified where the flow disconnected or broke down. Frank and his team worked hard to implement the changes required to fix the process.

In fact, after they finished, Frank was quite surprised about how much work it had taken to put the improvements in place. In his opinion, it had taken longer than expected to work through the process re-engineering. He couldn't quite put his finger on why, but he suspected it had to do with more than simply resistance to change. *Adaptability* had been identified as a key value in a previous current culture survey, and Frank judged his team to be quite adaptable.

However, Frank also understood that all the work in his division required a high level of teamwork to come together—perhaps more so than in any other company unit. He and his fellow executives had held deep debates on their desired corporate values. Along with adaptability, *teamwork* had emerged as one of the top values needed to drive the organization's success. But Frank knew many of his employees had *not* included teamwork as a value. That meant it didn't rank very high in the current culture survey.

To encourage employees to place more value on teamwork, Frank held several meetings with each of his units. He explained the importance of the process changes underway in the unit, saying how these changes would benefit the company's financial performance. He noted how critical the unit's performance was to delivering the company's goals. He even had posters with motivational teamwork slogans hung in the cafeteria and hallways.

Despite all these efforts, when the end of the year came around, not much had changed. Where was his high-performing team? He had emphasized the importance of teamwork, and given several speeches on how they needed to work together to achieve success and yet where was the teamwork needed to propel the unit forward?

In a last-ditch effort recommended by a colleague outside the company, Frank decided to measure the personal values of the employees in his unit via a values-assessment survey. To his surprise, teamwork did not register in the top 12 values of the employees, just as teamwork hadn't been included in the current culture survey. So if no one in the unit cared about teamwork, was it any surprise the team members didn't make any effort to work together?

Now Frank understood why his employees struggled to work as a team and why he constantly had to push them to get the work done. Yes, they'd attended the process reviews with the consultant, and yes, they'd somewhat adjusted the way they worked. After all, they were adaptable. Still, some days Frank felt like coaching his team was like pushing jelly up a wall. He had organized teamwork events, and they had dutifully showed up. But that's the thing about values. They represent the *core beliefs* and behaviors owned by every individual, not something that can be forced. It wasn't that Frank's employees *couldn't* work as a team or didn't value teamwork at all; it simply wasn't high on their list of priorities. Yet for Frank's area of operations, teamwork was a critical component.

Once Frank had a better understanding of the misalignment between his employees' personal values and the company's desired values, Frank could see that just hanging posters and holding barbeques wasn't enough to raise the bar on teamwork.

Missing Ingredient—Employees' Personal Values

So often when we work through cultural transformations,

we concentrate all our time on measuring the organization's current state and pushing it toward a future desired state. However, we rarely approach this process from the standpoint of our employees' personal values. Yet that missing perspective is like a missing ingredient; without it, you may have the meat, marinade, and fancy barbeque but no flame. You can improve the meat by adding the marinade, but you can't bring it to a sizzling completion until you understand how much heat you'll need.

However, if your employees' values are closely aligned to the organization's, they will want to come with you on the journey of cultural transformation. Even difficult journeys can be made less burdensome with the right planning, training, and support systems. If you embark on a quest to change your company culture without aligning personal values and corporate values, you'll feel like you're crossing the Sahara Desert without water.

Each of us forms our personal values based on our beliefs and experiences. Some of Frank's employees had previously had bad experiences when it came to teamwork, and those experiences had naturally jaded their viewpoints on its benefits. To view teamwork in a positive light, they would need to re-experience *firsthand* the personal benefits of being part of a team. Frank could best accomplish this through training as well as individual and team coaching. After all, not everyone is born with the ability to be a good team member. How many children have had to be taught over and over the concept of sharing? Just as children learn the reciprocal benefits of sharing and playing together, adults also need this training—and on-the-job coaching can be a powerful tool to achieve this.

The Role of Company Support

To encourage employees to adopt a new personal value, you need to ensure that your company's policies also support that value. In Frank's case, some of his employees valued the financial stability that comes with increased earnings. They had grown up with parents who had to scrimp, save, and work long hours to provide for their families. The company, however, used a remuneration reward system based on individual results. Each person's job had bonus criteria specific to that *individual* role. If employees produced the required output, they got rewarded—even if they trampled someone else along the way, didn't communicate with others, or refused to help in other areas. This misaligned policy did not reward good teamwork and therefore did not support the kind of culture managers desired.

Do you see why it's critical to include personal values when you measure your organization's culture? Doing so will help identify where your company's culture *really* stands and then allow you to accurately identify the changes needed to make a shift. It will also help you understand if you have the right people for your organization. Imagine trying to create an environment of innovation in which none of the employees value innovation! You would end up in Frank's position, doing all the "right" things but not reaping the full benefits. However, if you had a team with members who were energized by the thought of creating something new, innovation as a value would be less revolutionary—and would take far less effort to inspire.

The first step is to understand your own personal values (see next chapter). The second step is to understand the personal values of your employees. An aggregate view of your employees' values is a good start, but having an understanding of *each* employee helps even more. Doing some kind of personal values exercise in a workshop setting can help build cohesion in a department. It will also help you as a leader understand what motivates employees to be most productive.

When personal values line up with corporate values, things really start cooking.

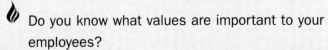

FUEL FOR THOUGHT

🔥 Do you know what values are important to your employees?

🔥 Have you measured the degree of your employees' personal alignment to your ideal corporate culture?

🔥 If you knew this, what ingredients could you add to foster high performance in that unit?

CHAPTER FOUR

The Building Blocks of Culture

To review, the building blocks of culture rest on a foundation of values. Each person has his or her core values made up of individual experiences, beliefs, and behaviors. Thus, it's important to understand our employees' personal values to affect a company-wide culture change.

A good first step is to look at ourselves. Surprisingly, few of us are fully aware of *our own* personal values until we're faced with a situation that forces us to dig deep.

My "aha" moment arrived in 1998. I was married with two teenage children, Diane, 16, and Geoff, 13. They were both active in sports, drama, and other after-school activities. At that time, I held a senior leadership role in the second largest division at Rogers Communications. With Ted Rogers at the helm, the company was at the leading edge of innovation and expansion. We were launching new products while also buying up adjacent cable systems. Keeping up with the demands on me at work was a huge task.

Then community service factored in. In addition to serving on several boards already, my job required me to be the face of Rogers in the community. I participated in multiple telethons and presented awards at business and school events. In addition, I constantly cultivated relationships with members of three levels of government as well as officials in the Canadian Radio and Television Commission, our industry's regulatory body.

"You have it all, Carol," people would exclaim. From their standpoint, I had a successful family, a top job, and a role that allowed me to hang out with the city's "who's who" at glamorous galas.

Don't get me wrong—a part of me loved all the interaction and the in-the-moment sense of contribution I enjoyed at each event. But the demands kept piling up. I became the poster child for saying yes to everything, believing it was good to feel needed.

However, the upward spiral of doing too much began to take its toll. The overwhelming storm continued to build, and even easy tasks became challenges. Activities that should have been fun and energizing became annoying and exhausting. I turned to alcohol and sleeping pills to try and calm the world around me.

Finally, I met my breaking point. I took a two-week leave to stop the insanity. That's when I began to examine the different pieces of my life. I loved my family and wouldn't leave them. Maybe a career change would turn things around. I had to do something!

Luckily, at the same time, I was working with an executive coach who helped me define my personal values. The focus I gained by being crystal clear about what's important to me was a stress reducer and a lifesaver. My values coming into sharp focus included integrity, family and friends, lifelong learning, and physical activity outdoors. Prioritizing these values helped me weather the storm and move forward.

Have you ever thought you were on the road to success, but trying to do too much led you off track?

It took me a long time to learn to say no. But when I did, amazingly, lightning didn't strike, friends and colleagues still talked to me, and my life did continue. My personal values became the goalposts for my journey. If an opportunity didn't fall between those goalposts, then it wasn't the right opportunity for me. As I became better and better at making choices that aligned with my personal values, joy and energy returned to my life. Simply stated, I spent less time on what didn't matter to me and more time on what did.

Overloaded World

In today's world, we tend to be bombarded with opportunities. We face a never-ending stream of emails in our electronic inboxes. In an article titled "Overloaded Circuits," Edward Hallowell talks about a new neurological disorder he calls Attention Deficit Trait (ADT). "ADT isn't an illness or character defect," he reports. "It's our brains' natural response to exploding demands on our time and attention." According to Hallowell, distractibility, inner frenzy, and impatience are all core symptoms.[1]

Define Core Personal Values

Knowing our personal values helps alert us when stress stems from a misalignment of those values. Once we know those values, we can address the stress in one of three ways. We can: 1) accept it as a short-term situation that will pass; 2) step up and change the situation to bring our values into alignment; or 3) walk away and leave the situation.

Want to define your core personal values? The following exercise will help you.

Step 1: Review the chart of words that follows. Read through the words and check off those that resonate with you. Remember, there are no right or wrong values. This isn't about which values you "think" you should have; it's a first step to finding out what's important to you. How you live with these values is a separate exercise. Select between 15 and 20 words, but don't over-think the assignment. If you think certain words are missing, feel free to add them to the list!

Personal Key Values

❑ Risk	❑ Grace	❑ Togetherness
❑ Impact	❑ Serve	❑ Empathize
❑ Design	❑ Learn	❑ Relate with God
❑ Sensations	❑ Guide	❑ Educate
❑ Expert	❑ Have fun	❑ Triumph
❑ Wealth	❑ Attractiveness	❑ Family
❑ Problem Solving	❑ Assist	❑ Support
❑ Imagination	❑ Locate	❑ Be passionate
❑ To glow	❑ Cause	❑ Instruct
❑ Honesty	❑ Sensual	❑ Score
❑ Gamble	❑ Being alone	❑ Harmony
❑ Stimulate	❑ Physical challenge	❑ Enlighten
❑ Conceive	❑ Uncover	❑ Win over
❑ Freedom	❑ Inspire	❑ Take risk
❑ Set standards	❑ Play games	❑ Loyalty
❑ Courage	❑ Quality	❑ Fame
❑ Encourage	❑ Improve	❑ Danger
❑ Assemble	❑ Magic	❑ Stability
❑ To feel good	❑ Influence	❑ Money
❑ Be entertained	❑ Venture	❑ Truth
❑ Coach	❑ Minister to	❑ Dominate field
❑ Innovation	❑ Locate	❑ Independence
❑ Community	❑ Power and authority	❑ Facilitate
❑ Competition	❑ Arts	❑ Privacy
❑ Faith	❑ Cooperation	❑ Experiment
❑ Travel	❑ Respect	❑ Creativity
❑ Accomplishment	❑ Peace	❑ Flexible work schedule

Step 2: Once you've checked off all the words that resonate with you, have a look at the selected ones. You'll likely see some trends in your selection. For example, you may have checked off a group of words that includes *stimulate, encourage, inspire,* and *educate*. For you, they may all connect with teaching and mentoring.

Use the following grid to sort through your words and discover the trends unique to you. Start this exercise by placing your first checked value into row one. Then consider the second checked value. Does it link to the first one or feel separate? If it feels linked, add it to row one. If it doesn't, place it on the second line to begin a second theme.

One by one, work through all the words until you've grouped them into a number of themes. Most people find they identify four to six.

	Trend /Theme
Example	*Stimulate, encourage, inspire, educate*
1	
2	
3	
4	
5	
6	

When you participate in activities that align with these themes, you'll likely find you feel less stress than usual. When you're working out of alignment, it's a good bet you'll notice a rise in your stress levels. If you work in a job that doesn't allow you to exercise at least some of your personal values, you'll find the job a chore. If you enjoy growing your staff, for example, and yet the company insists you spend all of your time cost cutting, you might need extra energy to focus on your work. On the other hand, if you grouped designing, problem solving, money, and stability as a theme, you may enjoy the challenge of cost cutting.

Step 3: The final step will help you remember your personal values. After all, if you're already bombarded with information, how can you possibly retain the 15–20 words that represent each theme? So let's name the themes instead; it's easier to remember four to six words than 20. You'll expand the chart from Step 2 to allow for this.

This exercise is simple. Just think of any person, place, or thing that describes your theme, and write it in.

	Trend /Theme	Theme Name
Example 1	*Stimulate, encourage, inspire, educate*	*Mr. Roberts (a high school teacher who inspired me)*
Example 2	*designing, problem solving, money, and stability*	*Abacus (an ancient tool used for counting)*

Now when you find yourself stressed or drained of energy, look at the situation and discover which one of your values you're *not* honoring. If you've spent the whole week in budget meetings and can't wait for the weekend, maybe it's because your "Mr. Roberts" value didn't get any attention this week.

Let's also be real here: It's highly unlikely you'll be perfectly aligned to your company's or another's values 100 percent of the time. However, being out of alignment for long periods can make life feel overwhelming.

FUEL FOR THOUGHT

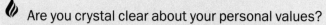 Are you crystal clear about your personal values?

 If you've taken on too much, what could you say no to?

 How aligned is your work to your personal values?

CHAPTER FIVE

Evolving Culture

"Life is a journey, not a destination." Have you heard this adage many times? Well, it applies to all aspects of our lives, including our work lives.

Our careers are all about the journey—a long-term evolving path and not a one-time arrival at a particular destination. When we do reach destinations along the way, we don't stop. In fact, our day-to-day activities usually support a variety of parallel journeys in different stages. Some journeys are in the planning stages. That's when we're assembling the necessary materials that allow us to embark on the journey. Others are off and running, traversing a continent of product development. Sometimes, we pause to reflect on the path we're taking, weighing the pros and cons of our experience and discovering how to enhance it even further. And for some—the visionaries and researchers—we explore new horizons, creating new journeys and interim destinations.

The world around us constantly evolves and so does our culture. The 1960s produced a free-spirited hippie counterculture. The 1970s saw women entering the workforce in greater numbers, as well as the ongoing influence of the women's movement and an anti-war movement. The 1980s introduced an era of "Me, Me, Me," with slogans such as "If you've got it, flaunt it" and "Shop 'til you drop." The 1990s saw the emergence of the electronic age with the birth of the Internet, which has changed the way we do things forever. And in the first decade of the 21st century, we experienced Y2K, globalization, a slew of natural and financial disasters, and the war on terrorism.

Corporate culture is no different from the culture that defines a decade; it's also influenced by events and leaders within our organizations. It will constantly evolve, either organically or by design. The shifting cultures of the times affect our businesses, so we constantly evolve to meet changing consumer, economic, and regulatory demands. If we concentrate on the destination, we get left behind. Making a change in our corporate culture must be seen as an evolving journey, not an overnight trip.

A Shift in Corporate Culture

I remember my first exposure to a shift in our company's corporate culture. I was a director in Ottawa for a company with several satellite offices. The executive leaders in Toronto had embarked on a "Corporate Culture Initiative." They conducted employee focus groups to help them come up with desired values. Once they had pulled together a short list, a survey was sent out to all employees and the final five desired corporate values were selected.

Then they sent a fancy, colorful communications package to each employee announcing the new values and providing a description of each. Along with one of my managers, Andy, I was selected to engage in a train-the-trainer program for leaders across the company. Once we completed our training, Andy and I visited all our satellite offices and held employee workshops—a fun time in our organization. In fact, fun was one of the values!

Specifically, we placed posters around the room describing each value and invited our employees to line up behind the value that resonated most for them. The workshops generated a lot of interesting discussion about the meaning of each of the new values. We followed these workshops by giving each employee a funky desktop ornament to remind everyone of these important values.

Then life went on. The priorities of the business took over, and corporate culture seemed to slide off the radar screen. Bit by bit, the emphasis on values drifted away. When it came time for a year-end recap, we reflected on how the values workshops had energized us—yet they'd become a distant memory. Some of us wondered if we would bring back those values in the coming year—or had we all just been experimenting with a new fad? It appeared we had arrived at a certain destination; the journey had ended.

Much later, I knew better. By that point, I had become a regional president running a large and successful region for the organization. In fact, out of the five regions, ours had the best employee engagement scores and the best performance metrics, including financial metrics. Finally, I was promoted to run the largest of the regions. How exciting!

Unfortunately, the largest region also showed the worst performance. So of course, the first order of the day was to assess current and desired cultures.

Running operational units requires them to be interdependent. No one can be successful with each department in a separate silo, hoarding information. Yet that described the environment I inherited. Under the current culture, employees blamed others for terrible results and denied that improvements could be made. The culture simply didn't support problem solving and working together; it was "every man for himself."

Over time, we put in place initiatives to shift the culture, removing some employees because their value systems didn't line up with where the organization wanted to go. We coached others on being okay with demonstrating values that had been suppressed by the previous leaders. To better align with work goals, we adjusted the organizational structure. We identified and dissected root causes for poor performance and quality, then planned and implemented incremental improvement programs. Along the way, we celebrated successes to ensure we continually reinforced this new way of working.

It proved to be a steady process; after all, an organization can only take so much change at once. Unless you're a professional juggler, trying to spin all the plates at the same time simply doesn't work. Over the course of three years, we continually managed toward our desired values and gradually transformed the organization.

And that new culture provided better results. We moved from a mediocre employee-satisfaction measure to a best-in-class score. Three years of process and performance improvements had built traction. The operational metrics had also improved, and our region was no longer at the bottom of the heap. When the process change uncovered a manual, Excel-based workforce management system that was unmanageable, we introduced a new automated system—bringing the organization up to par with external companies in the same industry. Such support mechanisms didn't exist previously.

Employees were able to hold their heads high, be proud of their accomplishments, and feel their opinions were valued.

The Alien Label

One of the most amazing transformations took place between the internal workforce and six external contracting firms. The initial culture assessment placed a lot of blame for problems on the "contractors." "They" were impossible to work with; "they" were shifty individuals you couldn't trust. This theme wound its way into many of our conversations during the day. Finally, I stepped in and asked why people kept referring to the contractors as if "they" were aliens dropping in from outer space every morning—doing "their" work and then piling back into the spaceship to head home to another planet. "Quite frankly, I'm surprised no one has commented on their green skin," I declared. A blanket of silence fell across the room. Finally, one woman piped up. "Maybe we should stop calling them contractors and come up with another name. Maybe we could call them business partners."

That one moment defined our behaviors toward the contracting firms for the next three years. At first, they didn't trust us; after all, the sudden change made it seem as if we'd all been drinking some sort of crazy potion. But over time, we built up a true relationship and worked to create one overall team, not an internal team versus an external team. Who would have known such a small name change—contractor to business partner—could have released so much opportunity for improvement? Having rebuilt the foundation of our business by creating a better culture, we were much better positioned to move the business forward.

Did we make it all the way to number one? Not quite. While we'd been working hard to shift the culture, other regions had continued to improve. It had taken time for our team to shift all the energy previously spent on blame and defensiveness and channel it into problem solving and teamwork. So while we'd caught up to the performance levels the other region had attained when we started our journey, they too had moved on. However, we had certainly closed the gap, and in the meantime, we'd contributed in a much more meaningful way to the overall success of the company. We had completed a leg in the journey, and we made sure to celebrate along the way.

Lifting Actions Off the Page

We've all had the experience of hiring consultants to help us resolve problems. Generally, they come in and do an assessment and define problems. Sometimes they even provide action items to resolve the issues. However, most businesses are unable to lift the action items off the page, out of the binder, and into reality.

The same is true of a cultural transformation. To be successful, it has to be more than a one-time checkmark in a box. To keep up with changing times, it needs to be an ongoing, living-and-breathing part of the business, and it requires a strategic plan. Plus, leaders wishing to engage in a shift in culture must have the strength and vision to use the map in the course of their everyday business. And just like other roadmaps, this one needs to be constantly reassessed against market changes, people changes, and business changes. A culture that supported baby-boomer values will not necessarily support Generation Y values. And conversely, a culture of "anything goes" is unlikely to survive in a world demanding personal and economic accountability.

The evolution of culture within a business starts by addressing the fundamental beliefs and behaviors of the people. Once this part of journey starts to fall into place, the energy becomes focused on positive outcomes. Moving the business forward no longer feels as if you're pushing a gigantic boulder uphill by yourself. Instead, momentum builds, and you and your employees are ready to meet any challenges that come your way.

FUEL FOR THOUGHT

How will you celebrate and maintain your momentum for lasting culture change—and not simply create the next fad in your company?

What tools do you need to pack as you continue your journey?

Where will you find additional support and strength to lead your company through ongoing changes in the business world around you?

CHAPTER SIX

Poor Culture,
Poor Company

Having a great culture isn't only about motivating employees. Financial benefits come with it, too. Lousy culture comes with a price tag. By improving productivity and reducing costs, a strong culture can become a competitive advantage.

After all, you may be already worn down by year after year of cost cutting. Perhaps every budget cycle brings back the mantra of "do more with less." Maybe you've flattened your organization by taking out layers of management, scaled back to focus on core competencies, or reduced travel costs by implementing virtual meetings and conference calls. Maybe you've gone so far as to cut employee training or employee recognition events that involve parties and celebrations. (Even providing coffee and donuts became a no-no at our 7 a.m. group technician meetings before the technicians headed out on the road for the day!) Eventually, you run out of options and become frustrated by the constant demand to find more areas to cut.

Perhaps you recognize that one of the most visible costs of a terrible corporate culture is high employee turnover, which results in increased hiring and training costs. Have you taken time to measure in hard dollars these costs to your business? If it's highly labor-intensive, the numbers can be staggering.

Beyond this, productivity costs can be associated with bureaucratic or fragmented cultures in which employees don't feel empowered. However, the number of businesses looking at and calculating these costs is in the minority. What should companies focus on when they're trying to cost out the impact of their poor corporate culture?

Elements of a "Bad" Culture

The first step is to identify the elements of a "bad" culture. Several models have tried to define the values that contribute in a negative way to the performance of an organization. Whether we call them "limiting" or "negative" values, they drag a business down rather than propel it forward. You can build the best racecar in the world and hire highly trained drivers. However, if there's sludge in the fuel, your race is destined for mechanical failure.

Is there sludge in your corporate fuel that's slowing the pace of your organization? When does the amount of sludge cause you to lose your competitive edge—not only from a speed standpoint but from the standpoint of what it costs to run your race team? How can you make sure the substances going into your fuel are driving performance, while you eliminate substances that are actually creating sludge?

At Rogers, we thought our division was performing pretty well. Then our company undertook an overall cultural assessment. When we received the results and reviewed the inventory of values, we discovered among them a few limiting values. To our surprise, bureaucracy, finger-pointing, blame, and inward focus all made the list. But in the culture employees identified as desirable, we saw the opposite values: empowerment, teamwork, and customer focus.

We realized that acting on these results could have significant effects on our costs and revenues. Clearly, if we shifted more of our inwardly focused energy to customer service, we could improve customer satisfaction and loyalty. Better customer retention would open up the possibility to upsell more customers, improving our average revenue per customer. We could reduce the number of customer complaints coming into our call center, also reducing the resources required for follow-up service calls.

When we dug deeper, we found even more cost impacts. Our employees estimated that they were spending almost 15 percent of their time doing paperwork, managing circulation of documents for approval, and writing daily status reports. In addition, every week they sat through four-hour meetings recapping the prior week's activities in excruciating detail. What happened to all those reports? A whole tier of managers spent *their* time collecting and reviewing reports, only to pass them further up the organization. We had checkers checking the checkers in order to make sure that when directors presented their reports, they incurred no risk of someone else at the table contradicting them.

Finally, we identified another alarming misuse of time: the total hours employees spent in coffee or smoke breaks, gossiping about co-workers or complaining about problems and barriers. When Fatima, our accountant, brought me the time-study results, the dollar value of the time employees spent grumbling was more significant than I'd even dared to imagine. Previously, I'd been charged with developing cost-saving programs, and we'd been digging madly through ways to improve process or performance. Suddenly, I knew the cost of the company's limiting values—a gold mine by comparison! Clearly, we'd been digging in the wrong place.

It was impossible to ignore such an analysis. This wasn't fluffy stuff; we'd been throwing real, measurable dollars down the drain. So we added values into our strategic planning process and created a new plan with a long-term emphasis. We recognized that if we did it right and made the change sustainable, we could save costs beyond a one-time hit and *permanently* improve bottom-line profits.

If we wanted to move away from bureaucracy, blame, and inward focus, we had to develop ongoing support for this change. We also knew that, to effect meaningful change, we had to move our employees from merely being aware of the need to making a long-term commitment to adopt the change. We incorporated these plans into our three-year budgeting process. Ultimately, we successfully shifted the culture, reduced costs, *and* improved customer satisfaction. This was one of the largest win-win initiatives we'd ever completed!

Cost of Limiting Values

Too often, leaders underestimate the impact of limiting values in their organization. When it comes to putting dollars in the budget for programs focused on culture improvements that will ultimately result in cost savings, these initiatives are rarely on the radar. Indeed, leaders often regard changing the culture as something they *should* do to boost employee satisfaction and reduce employee churn. Yes, improving culture certainly has these benefits, but it's clearly worth the effort to attach a financial cost to limiting values.

The cost doesn't need to be accurate down to the last penny. Believe me, it will be plenty large enough when you get through with the analysis. In our case, when we calculated 20 percent of inefficient time on a base of 400 employees at an average hourly rate of $20, the cost was more than $2.5 million a year! And while it's unrealistic to think any company could eliminate *all* inefficient time, you can imagine what a difference it would make to even cut it by half.

When hospital directors in the southern United States went through this exercise, they found that one of the hospital's largest costs was labor—and they also had significant costs for recruiting and training due to high employee turnover. Yes, they could have programs in place to improve employee retention through increased bonus programs or highly competitive salaries. However, money wasn't the main source of dissatisfaction or root cause for turnover. The hospital suffered from a poor culture, defined by lack of respect, relentless cost cutting, and mistrust. When the directors took on the culture issue, they reduced their employee churn from 24 percent to 15 percent. In another case, a bank focused on its limiting values and improved employee satisfaction from 49 percent to 85 percent over five years.

Addressing your limiting values not only effectively reduces business costs and makes a long-term, sustainable shift in your cost structure; it can also provide opportunities for increased revenues. And in a culture full of positive values, achieving these additional revenues takes much less effort. If your employees value customer service and want to work in an environment that supports customer service, they will naturally provide that customer service. In the end, changing culture is much more efficient than trying to improve customer service with top-down directives, command-and-control management procedures, and punishment-based programs to measure and manage performance.

Addressing your limiting values is a root-cause analysis. It gets to foundational issues rather than quick fixes, which is like simply putting additives into your existing fuel system. Instead of dreaming up nickel-and-dime, one-time cost savings programs such as eliminating travel or employee events, make the time to analyze the costs of your limiting values. Once you've completed an assessment of your current corporate culture, call out those limiting or negative values. Perform interviews within your organization to learn how these behaviors translate into lost productivity, turnover, and customer churn. Create a list of all the effects you collect and work through an exercise to add a dollar value to each cost.

Figure 6.1 provides an example of a limiting-values cost worksheet. Again, does it have to be accurate down to the last penny? No. The point of the exercise is not to try and justify every last dollar; it's to discover how your corporate culture is driving or holding back performance.

Limiting-Values Cost Worksheet

Limiting Values	How do they show up in our organization?	What's the cost?
Bureaucracy	Five levels of sign-off for items over $50K. Each level of sign-off requires 30 minutes to obtain. Four people work full time just moving documents through the approval process. Average length of time to obtain all approvals is three weeks, delaying implementation times.	25 documents per month x 30 minutes of executive time + four FTEs (Full-time employees). If half the proposals could be implemented within one week instead of three weeks, the incremental cost savings would be $XX.
Inward focused	Everyone focuses on defending his or her work rather than focusing on the customer. Customer complaints take almost a week to resolve because no one takes accountability. Instead, employees just pass the complaint around so that 100 complaints per week pass through five departments. It takes approximately 15 FTEs to handle these complaints. Additional credits get applied to customer accounts because customers become frustrated with the length of time it takes to correct a problem.	52,000 complaints, with an additional $20 credit applied to half of them = $520K. 15 FTEs @ $80K (fully loaded costs including benefit costs) = $1.2M

Figure 6.1 Limiting-Values Cost Worksheet

Working through your limiting values identifies the sludge slowing down your team. Once you've established the actual annual costs of your culture weaknesses, you'll have even more incentive to make changes.

Imagine the competitive impact you can make when you improve the culture of your organization while reducing your costs by six or seven figures! Without the sludge, you'll have created a high-octane fuel capable of launching your company out of the middle of the pack.

FUEL FOR THOUGHT

🔥 Do you know if your current culture contains any limiting or negative values?

🔥 How could those limiting values be affecting the performance of your organization, creating sludge in your corporate fuel?

🔥 What are the costs of your culture's limiting values?

CHAPTER SEVEN

Fueling Your Brand

Branding a company is an exercise to differentiate your organization and attract customers. Some people leap at the opportunity to break out the colored pens and draw logos and taglines rather than sit around the boardroom table coming up with another list of cost-saving ideas. Culture is a critical component of branding; in fact, there's no question the two are inextricably linked—and in many more ways than you might expect. For a company to be truly successful, branding and culture must be congruent with each other.

For example, a snappy tagline can motivate employees as much as it motivates customers. Remember Ford's famous tagline from the 1980s, "Quality is Job 1"? Beyond telling Ford's customers to associate motor products with quality, some would also argue it set the tone for Ford's employees to make quality the number-one value in their culture. What if you brand your company as number one in customer experience, yet customer experience doesn't show up in your corporate values? Your customers will find a disconnect when they call your customer care center and the phone representative is more worried about his or her average handle-time than providing a top-notch experience. Situations like this can keep customers from trusting a company's brand for a long time.

Many years ago, before the Internet, companies tended to operate more locally, with the customer base in the same region as the organization. Company leaders were also community leaders. Organizations were smaller, and it was common for workers to socialize together. Ideally, your corporate culture *was* your brand because your leader set the tone in the company and in the community.

Today, though, organizations are increasingly more global. With the rise of the Internet and e-commerce, a company can sell goods or services around the world. As the customer base broadens, the intimacy once shared between customer and business has started to dissipate. As customers, we often feel like another number in a long list of accounts. Virtually every company I do business with today starts the conversation by asking for my "number." Airlines want my frequent flyer number; gas stations want my credit card number; the ATM wants my bank card number and my PIN; and everyone wants my phone number and email.

On the plus side, we no longer need to go to a local provider when we can order products by phone or online. And the number of vendors has soared astronomically. But as all the available buying solutions bombard consumers, our job as branders becomes even more important—to cut through that clutter and differentiate our product from others.

Culture Supports Your Brand

Just as culture supports your strategies, culture will support your brand. Many companies have an unconscious culture and an unconscious brand. If you haven't declared your culture or your brand, others will do it for you. Your employees will be happy to tell you what they think the current culture is, and your customers will be happy to tell you what they think your company brand is. Assessing your culture and assessing your brand status follow similar methodologies except that one audience is internal and the other is external.

So how do the two work together?

In 1996, SageData developed one of the first barcode asset-tracking systems. Its inventor Patti Pokochak had the challenge of naming the new product.

One night while lying in bed reading the classic marketing book *Positioning: The Battle for your Mind* by Al Reis and Jack Trout, Patti kept repeating the words "bar code asset tracking" to brainstorm a clever name. She looked down at her two dogs snuggled at her feet, and a name suddenly came to her: BASSET, for **Ba**r Code **Asset** tracking system. The name played on the analogy of a tracking dog, turning a cold technology into something more fun for customers.

Next, the same company invented the Warehouse Information System that became the Whippet. Basset and Whippet systems ended up all over North and South America, Europe, Mauritius . . . and they've even been used for tracking battle tanks in Bosnia.

With these products, SageData had two branding success stories. But what made this organization even more successful? The congruency between its fun branding style and the small company's culture. While the employees were innovative technology engineers, as a group they also valued fun. When they went out to talk to clients, their passion for their products suited the creatively named systems. As the company grew, ex-clients wanted to join the company because they loved the culture the employees exuded whenever they discussed, installed, or maintained branded products and services.

There's no question that how your company looks on the inside will have an impact on how it's perceived on the outside. Take Johnson & Johnson as an example. Its branding conveys a consistent message, describing its products using the following words:

Baby care—products for the ones you love

Skin and hair care—trusted personal care products for your skin and hair

Nutritionals—products for a healthier diet

The Johnson and Johnson brand creates an emotion of trust and communicates that people in the company care about their customers' well-being. From a culture perspective, Johnson & Johnson's credo puts customers first. So while its external brand is about customer trust, the internal brand or culture also focuses on the customer. The company's leaders have tested this culture several times to ensure they balance their commitment to customers and patients with their commitment to shareholders.

Benchmark Branding Cases

Johnson & Johnson's handling of a tampering incident involving its product Tylenol is often cited as a benchmark branding case. In 1982, seven individuals died as a result of the deliberate contamination of Tylenol with cyanide. The tampered bottles came from a variety of manufacturing plants and yet the deaths all occurred in Chicago, leading to the conclusion that the tampering had not happened within Johnson & Johnson's manufacturing facilities. To this day, the culprit has not been identified and the case remains open. At the time, Tylenol represented close to 15 percent of the company's assets. CEO William Weldon knew that pulling this product off the market would result in a huge financial hit for the company, yet he did just that.

In fact, he went even further, halting production of the popular painkiller until the company's manufacturing system could produce industry-reforming tamper-resistant packaging. Weldon set the tone from the top about the importance of the customer and safety. Shareholder value fell in line behind these values. Johnson & Johnson took a financial hit, but the company recovered due to the strength of its brand and the congruency of its culture.

In contrast, consider the story of BP and the Gulf of Mexico oil spill in April 2010. Over the years, BP had completed a number of branding exercises. In 2003, its leaders announced the new marketing message "Beyond Petroleum," meant to signal that the company valued social responsibility in addition to oil production. The logo, a bright yellow sun surrounded by green, was designed to subtly remind consumers of earth and vegetation as well as to align oil with other organic products of nature. By drawing on such environmentally friendly imagery, BP attempted to make consumers feel good about using oil in their everyday lives. The marketing proved successful, and BP became one of the top global oil brands.

Then in 2010, disaster struck. When a BP oil rig exploded in the Gulf of Mexico and claimed 11 lives, the fiery images quickly spread through the international media. Those first images were later followed by underwater camera footage showing the unbridled flow of oil into the ocean. BP's management came under question, from everyday conversations to Congressional hearings. Worse, the media soon reminded the public this wasn't BP's first deadly and damaging disaster.

In March 2005, one of BP's refineries in Texas had caught fire, and the ensuing explosion killed 15 employees and injured 170 others. A year later, in March 2006, BP pipelines in Alaska spilled more than 200,000 gallons of oil onto Alaska's wild tundra because of a leak at Purdue Bay oilfields. According to Environmental Protection Agency attorney Jeanne Pascal, BP had been fined hundreds of millions of dollars and charged with four federal crimes over the years.

With the massive spill in the Gulf of Mexico, BP's brand promise of environmental responsibility leaked to the bottom of the ocean floor. The incident incited a large public outcry, including many environmental groups. In fact, Greenpeace directly targeted BP's brand, organizing a logo parody contest that produced the following images.[2]

The misalignment of brand promise and corporate culture at BP contributed to this demise. The responsible pledge of "Beyond Petroleum" clearly didn't reflect the internal workings of the company. Despite massive fines for failure to operate in a safe environment, safety was never a top value. The cost to repair all the safety violations was seen to be more expensive than the fines. Shutting down operations to make the necessary safety improvements would impede other higher priorities like speed of delivery. According to a Gulf of Mexico rig survivor interviewed on the TV news magazine *60 Minutes*, BP ordered partners to cut corners because their absurdly ambitious drill schedule was off by several weeks. Clearly, the company was not focused on social and environmental responsibility. Instead, it was highly focused on profits and cost effectiveness.[3]

To make matters worse, in the weeks and months that ensued, BP also demonstrated a culture of blame. They started by blaming the Gulf of Mexico oil spill on their contractors—not unlike their reaction to the Texas refinery incident, where they first pointed fingers at "employee error." Not once did they connect the spill's causes with management actions or decisions. To add insult to injury, they delayed too long before making any announcements about the company's accountability.

Brands are External; Culture is Internal

Much more can be said about the culture at BP and the impact on its operations. What's important to understand is the difference between brands and culture. Brands are external. Whether you're in the barcode software business, the health care sector, or the oil industry, your brand describes a promise to your customers. Culture, on the other hand, is internal. It's not about logos and taglines; it's about values, behaviors, and the way work gets done.

In the cases of SageData and Johnson & Johnson, the culture is congruent with the brand. These companies' brands can flourish on the solid foundation of their top cultural values. On the other hand, BP's culture revealed itself to be so misaligned with its brand, that the brand might never recover and the company's reputation has suffered great damage. Clearly, the Gulf of Mexico oil spill hurt the company financially. But imagine the other long-term internal consequences, such as the recruitment nightmare that must have followed the disaster. Who wants to work for a company that puts profits before the lives of their employees?

Whenever you engage in a branding exercise, don't just get caught up in the fun of playing with taglines and logos. It's critical to ask the questions: "Does our culture support this brand promise? Do our internal behaviors make it easy to deliver the marketing message we're sending to our customers?"

If your brand and culture are not aligned, your employees will become confused, and so will your present and potential customers. If employees hear the mantra, "The customer is number one"—except when their call-handle time exceeds the target—they aren't sure which way to turn, and performance suffers. The best companies ensure the integrity and authenticity of their brands by keeping culture and branding on parallel paths.

FUEL FOR THOUGHT

- Does your culture support your brand?
- What questions do you need to ask your marketing and executive teams to make sure your culture and brand align with each other?
- How authentic is your brand?

CHAPTER EIGHT

The IGNITE Process

Having the right corporate culture can launch a business ahead of the competition. And while corporate culture doesn't need to be rocket science, at times it may certainly feel like it. Effective planning is like building and launching a space shuttle. Preferably, the most demanding logistical work comes during the design, fueling, and lift-off of the rocket. Once the rocket ship breaks through gravity, the journey itself should run smoothly.

The same is true for our organizational culture. When you can tweak certain systems or processes or try to motivate your employees with posters, essentially you are just dropping additives into your organizational fuel. However, dropping additives into today's corporate fuel just isn't enough to propel our businesses forward. We need to do a complete fuel analysis and rocket ship design. Our corporate fuel draws on the power of our employees, and the rocket ship design reflects our process, procedures, and policies. You won't get results if you use water to fuel a rocket or pour rocket fuel into a Vespa. The fuel and vehicle design must align in order to achieve maximum performance.

Okay, now it sounds like we're getting back to rocket science, but even rocket science can be broken down into manageable parts. The IGNITE process is designed to break down the elements needed to improve your culture. By following these six steps you can take today's culture and shift it in a way that will power your people, profits and potential.

1. I = Inquire
2. G= Gather
3. N= Name
4. I= Imbed
5. T = Track
6. E=Evaluate

I for Inquire

During this first step you will use proven assessment tools to get a baseline on your current culture. It's important to survey all levels in your organization along with relevant demographic splits. For example, if your organization has multiple locations, understanding the culture at each site is important. Leaders in each site may be managing differently resulting in different cultures. If your company is organized by function, you will want the survey information to determine the cultures by functional leader. Having a view of the culture from various levels within the organization will help determine how well the leader's message is reaching down into the organization. As the CEO, you may believe your culture is one way, and yet your front-line employees may have a very different perspective.

Knowing where you are today is the fuel analysis part of the process. Now you know what you're starting with. You can see if there is corporate sludge in your fuel or not.

G is for Gather

This is the follow-up phase to Inquire. The two go hand in hand; however, they are very specific and separate activities. This is where you use your survey information to open up conversations about what's really going on in the organization. Just getting the data isn't enough. Understanding the data is critical. And so you need to go deep into the organization through focus groups or follow-up surveys to collect the stories behind the data. If confusion shows up in your current culture, what does that actually mean? How does confusion show up in the organization?

Bill and Sam, co-owners of a medium-sized pharmaceutical service, decided to review their corporate culture. They sent out a communication to their 300 employees announcing an online survey to find out what people thought about the current culture and where people would like to see changes. When they sat down and reviewed the words employees used to describe the company, Bill picked out one word in particular: fun. He wondered what the word "fun" really meant in the context of his company. Did it mean people were dancing in the hallways and shooting Nerf balls at each other? That didn't sound like a team focused on delivering to customers. Or did it just mean that employees found the work environment relaxed, open, and enjoyable? By holding focus groups with his employees Bill was better able to understand the various perspectives that people had on fun.

It may be tempting to start thinking and talking about ways to solve issues, and one should certainly collect ideas that come up. First, however, you need to get a very thorough viewpoint on the current situation. During this phase, you can also start costing the financial impact of culture on your organization. For example, how is confusion preventing people from being fully productive? When you ask employees how confusion shows up in the organization, they may give examples of having to spend time getting clarifications over and over again because their managers aren't able to properly communicate. How often do they need to seek out additional clarifications? How many employees are asking the same questions, individually, which eats up the manger's time too?

N is for Name.

Having spent some time reflecting on where your organization is today, you can develop the culture recipe for where you need to be in order to be more successful. Naming the ingredients or values to your desired culture occurs during this phase. You will want to come up with three to five core values that are essential to the business. If you have an operation like I had at Rogers, teamwork will likely be one of those key core values. If you are in an industry where innovation is what drives business growth, then innovation will be one of your key values. In some cases, these values may already exist in your current culture. In other cases, you may need to declare new values in order to improve your situation. No one wants to have confusion in their culture, so if it shows up in your current culture, you will want to replace it with something else like open communications.

Sometimes, however, you may need to take some interim steps. It's very difficult to move from blame to teamwork in one step. When I was faced with this situation, employees needed respect before they were willing to go to teamwork. Teamwork was the ultimate goal, but we settled on respect during our first rendition of the desired culture.

In our previous example, Bill and Frank decided that fun was a value that needed to be in their recipe of core values. But without a full description of the ingredient, the recipe still wasn't clear. If a recipe lists sugar as an ingredient, does it mean white sugar, brown sugar, refined sugar, or something else? To clarify their list of ingredients, Bill and Sam created roundtable forums with a cross section of their employees. With several groups of eight employees, they discussed the words the employees had selected. In animated conversations, the employees described their interpretations of each word. They seemed to generate as many different perspectives as they had words! It was clear each person's perspective drew from the experiences and personal values unique to that individual. However, what the groups did find was that while words may have different meanings to different people, once they aggregated those words into themes, a common meaning emerged. When "fun" was grouped with "respect," "creativity," and "teamwork," Bill better understood what his employees were asking for. And the employees could describe this ingredient in more detail: "Fun—the respectful humor and joy each of us brings to our team. It helps us to be positive and productive."

I is for Imbed

Imbedding the desired values into your organization requires more than just words on the wall. This is where a lot of the heavy lifting takes place. Having defined the ingredients of the fuel during the first three phases, now the actual creation of that fuel takes place. You will develop a list of initiatives to correct or improve your culture. Likely there will be a large number of ideas that can be collected from all levels within the organization. They will be people related, process related, policy related, and even systems related. All of this information then needs to be prioritized. Trying to do too much too quickly doesn't serve anyone. The change in the organization must be manageable and sustainable. This is where having a blueprint for action can be helpful. You can map out your initiatives and see how the implementation phases of the various projects have an impact on different parts of the organization. It will also help set expectations for how quickly the shift in culture can take place.

As Sam and Bill worked on naming the values for their core value recipe, they also realized that some ingredients in the current culture had gone bad. "Bureaucracy" was one of those areas. As the company had grown, some of its processes hadn't kept up. Peggy in purchasing complained about the manual system for purchase order creation and tracking: "Sam, did you know I spend so much time creating, filing, and copying purchase orders, I'm going to need an assistant next year? I'd rather be spending my time sourcing out better pricing and delivery options than filing and photocopying. That stuff just isn't fun."

Bill made a note to add an automated purchasing system to their plans. He collected many more employee ideas about processes and policies that contributed to bureaucracy. It wasn't a matter of changing a behavioral ingredient, as people weren't bureaucratic by nature. Instead, he needed to make changes to the current organizational blueprint.

Two months later, Bill and Sam sat down with Helen from finance, Ted from human resources, and Joshua from operations to review their three-year plan. Bill presented his list of employee ideas about things the company could do better. These ideas included ways to get rid of limiting values like bureaucracy by improving systems, processes, and policies. Together, the team mapped out what changes should be made and when. After all, advancements such as purchasing and implementing a new automated purchase-order system would require other changes as well.

Bill and Sam re-mapped the three-year plan, factoring in all the agreed-upon changes and their implications. Finally, they had a blueprint for the organization—the guidelines to build out an improved company. It also made sure incremental changes stayed aligned with the long-term strategic plan. No point in installing an automated purchase-order system if outsourcing purchasing was a better option.

Trying to change culture without a blueprint is like trying to sell a product without a marketing plan. Sure, you can try to do it based on current trends. But to be sustainable, you have to have a plan. At the same time, you have to ensure your plan stays integrated with your day-to-day business and can adapt to changing conditions within the organization. Like Captain Kirk of the Starship Enterprise, leaders need to know what courses to plot as well as which thrusters to activate and when.

T is for Track

We all know that what gets measured gets managed. To lift your initiatives off the paper, you and your leadership team need to accept the accountability to lead them. Creating a dashboard to track the progress of the various actions is incredibly helpful. This is where each activity can be broken down into milestones, and dates can be attached to each milestone. By tracking things this way, you can easily see if things start to slip off the rails. It also breaks some seemingly huge projects into a series of mini projects.

These projects can be mapped onto a specific culture calendar, or they can be integrated into other existing corporate dashboards. Either way, reviewing the progress on a regular basis will ensure the sustainability of the change.

E is for Evaluate

As we've seen in Chapter 5, cultures don't change overnight. It's a process of evolution. Expecting your culture to suddenly change overnight is unrealistic. You need to implement change and you need to let that change anchor itself in your organization. Likely, your culture calendar will spread over several years. However, at an appropriate time, perhaps around the 18-month point, you'll want to go back into the organization and evaluate the impact of the initiatives you have put in place. Have they had the desired effect in improving your culture? By running the same survey tool you used at the beginning, you can track your progress against the baseline results.

Over the course of the next three years, Sam and Bill used their recipe and blueprint, lifted ideas off the page, and created an improved culture for their company. Once a year, they re-assessed the culture. They were pleased to see bureaucracy slide to the bottom of the list of company values, eventually disappearing altogether. People became less frustrated with day-to-day obstacles. Their productivity increased and they grew as a team. A focus on cost reduction was gradually replaced with a focus on continuous improvement. So while employees maintained their connection to fun and teamwork and preserved their strong financial and customer-focused foundations, they also became more forward-thinking.

Bill and Sam's business successfully surged forward. The cost of bureaucracy had been eliminated from their financials, and continuous improvement manifested in better customer service and higher productivity. A couple of their competitors noticed that Sam and Bill increasingly beat them out on contracts. When asked for the secret, Sam and Bill just smiled and attributed their success to the great people in their organization.

These two leaders understood that playing with additives and tweaking things from time to time wouldn't be enough to thrust the company forward. At the same time, they also found out they didn't need to undergo a full redesign. What did work for them was analysis and documentation of the values held by their employees—the fuel of the organization—combined with compatible upgrades to their systems, processes, procedures, and policies. Integrating these two key elements into the strategic plan created a powerful organization with increased traction for the future. It wasn't rocket science after all—but it took a lot of hard work just to get to the launch pad. Remember: Every step along the way builds toward the next, and once your rocket is in space, all that hard work lifts you above the rest.

FUEL FOR THOUGHT

- Are you ready to move your organization to the launch pad?

- How can adopting the IGNITE process benefit your company?

- What resources will you need to help you through the IGNITE process?

CHAPTER NINE

I is For Inquire

The process of creating a culture that allows employees and the organization to grow into their full potential begins by asking the right questions. As Vanessa Redgrave once said, "Ask the right questions if you're going to find the right answers." Asking the right questions during the Inquire phase of the IGNITE process is what sets you on the path to making the right changes to your organization. Many leaders think the right questions are those meant to determine their employees' level of engagement. This may have been true in the past, but today we know there are better questions to get at the true nature of culture.

The building blocks of culture are values. So why not ask questions related directly to values? Let's cut to the chase. Many of the assessment tools out there still go at it indirectly or remain focused on employee engagement. As media analyst Marshall McLuhan once said, "Our Age of Anxiety is, in great part, the result of trying to do today's job with yesterday's tools and yesterday's concepts."

To find the right tools, it helps to find the right expert—for our purposes, a thought leader in the business world. We need an expert who offers how-to, not just theory. Let me introduce you to Richard Barrett. Like Peter Drucker and Jim Collins, Richard Barrett is an insightful business leader, and corporate culture is his area of expertise. He's the creator of the internationally recognized Cultural Transformation Tools (CTT) currently being used in 80 countries to support more than 6,000 organizations and leaders in their transformational journeys. He is the author of several powerful books on leadership.

I can liken my introduction to Richard to my introduction to my first dishwasher, a new tool that appeared in our home during a major kitchen upgrade. When Dennis and I were first married, washing dishes for the two of us was nothing. Admittedly, during university we simply stacked dirty dishes until there were no clean dishes left, but as a married couple, we became more disciplined in our nightly cleanup. Going to visit the in-laws, who came with a large family, meant cleaning up and washing dishes, which took on a whole new level of social interaction. Typically, my mother-in-law, my sisters-in-law, and I congregated in the kitchen for the wash-up. My father-in-law, my husband, and my brothers-in-law congregated in the front room. I felt transported back to the 1800s when the men retired to drink brandy and smoke cigars, leaving the women behind.

As we transitioned from a childless couple to parents, we faced many more dishes to wash. Finally, the impetus for change had arrived; we purchased a dishwasher. After the first week, of course we asked ourselves why we had waited so long and resisted making the investment. Clearly, the new tool had quelled our ongoing argument over who would do the dishes. It allowed us to focus on our family and other things that mattered more. The next family gift to our parents? A dishwasher!

During my career, I've encountered a lot of business tools. In the late 1990s, Kaplan and Norton's Balanced Scorecard changed the way we managed our businesses. In the 2000s, Harter, Schmidt, and Hayes's research on measuring employee engagement taught me that measuring the loyalty of our employees would further our organization's interest. When employee engagement became one of our key business indicators, some felt fearful about the new tool. Leading up to the survey, many of us engaged in employee-friendly events in the hopes this would translate into positive results. Introducing new tools into our environments can be a blessing, but it can also make us apprehensive. As leaders, we must overcome such fears and take advantage of the tools that can move our organizations forward.

Before Richard Barrett came along, many of us struggled to understand why some of our divisions performed better than others. The concept of corporate culture just wasn't on our radar screen. And yet, as I developed high-performing teams, I knew *how* we did things was just as important as *what* we did. My passion for learning more about that "how" got me an invitation to a session with Barrett during one of his rare trips to Canada from the UK. I remember sitting in the basement of a tall hotel in a cramped conference room with about 150 other leaders squeezed around the tables. Most of us had never heard Richard speak before. When he did, his propositions intrigued me. As the session proceeded and he described his methodology, I felt the same way I felt the day our dishwasher was hooked up. That day, he demonstrated an easy-to-use tool that would change the way our company worked. Instead of arguing over measuring our culture, we could now focus instead on making the right changes within our organization.

What an "aha" moment! Until then, I hadn't even realized how much I still struggled to get my arms around all this "culture" stuff. I knew when it didn't feel right, and I knew when it felt great. I had fumbled my way through using various facilitators, which seemed to yield okay results. However, here, finally, was someone with a model and methodology to explain corporate culture concepts that had still been fuzzy in my mind. Understanding his work simplified the exercise of collecting and synthesizing information, and trying to figure out how to deal with the results. With the help of this tool, we'd be able to see immediately where the organization stood.

Barrett's work is based on the familiar laws of Abraham Maslow's Hierarchy of Needs. Barrett translated the five Maslow levels of need into seven levels of organizational consciousness. As one gains proficiency in the lower levels, one can raise his or her consciousness to the next level. Barrett also applied a series of values to each level of consciousness. Finally, his tool for measuring company culture applies employees' chosen values to these seven levels. It's that simple; no complicated fuzzy descriptors for culture here.

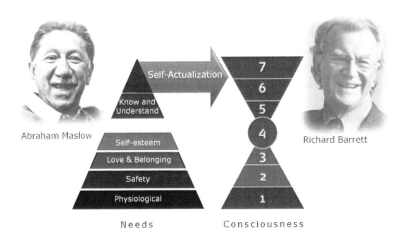

Figure 9.1 Derivation of Consciousness Model[4]

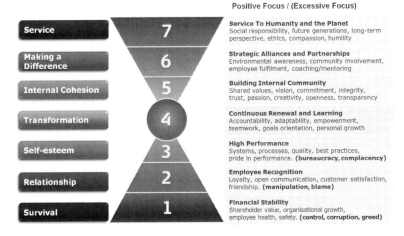

Figure 9.2 The Seven Levels of Consciousness[4]

As we've seen, values are the building blocks of culture. So how do values line up in this model?

The first level, survival, translates to financial stability. Just as we can't survive as humans without heat and food, we can't survive long in today's competitive environment without financial stability. Once our survival is assured, we can begin to look beyond ourselves and develop relationships—which translate to employee recognition at level two on Barrett's chart. At this level, we see the values that help us communicate with and acknowledge our employees. At level three—self-esteem—we start to strive to be better, as individuals and as organizations. Self-esteem corresponds to high performance. We continue this growth through level four—transformation (which corresponds to continuous renewal and learning)—and then we start to look externally. We embrace collaborations and alliances in levels five and six, internal cohesion and external cohesion. At level seven, service, we engage in work for the betterment of all.

Take Bill Gates as an example. He long ago surpassed the first level, financial stability. He created an organization and continually evolved himself and Microsoft through levels two to five—and arguably to level six. Now, as an individual, he operates at level seven through his foundation to "enhance healthcare and reduce poverty."

Note that the goal isn't to operate only at level seven and leave the other levels behind. Without financial stability, you can't solve world hunger. However, if you have people who value community, collaboration, and innovation in an organization that's focused solely on shareholder value, you won't be able to hold on to those people. In order to bring your passion to your work, your workplace's values must be similar to your own.

When you start the journey to create your organization's recipe, use the Barrett model to assess your employees' personal values and the current culture of your organization, as well as take a temperature check on your employees' desired culture. These assessments map directly, with no intermediate steps. There's no need to translate management styles, communication styles, or personality types. In one fell swoop, you'll get a visual into what your employees care about, where you are today, and where your employees want to be. These answers stem from three questions: (1) What's important to you? (2) How is your organization behaving today? (3) How would you like the organization to be tomorrow? All three questions specifically reference values.

In addition, the model defines positive and negative or limiting values. These limiting values are the low-hanging fruit when you want to improve your culture and, ultimately, your organization's performance. Limiting values may be people-related values like "control" or they may be process-related values like "bureaucracy."

Let's follow CEO Chuck, his leadership team, and his employees as they use this assessment tool to inquire about their organization.

Step 1: The CEO Assessment

The CEO completes the assessment that measures his or her personal values and perception of the current values in the organization as well as the values he or she believes are required to make the organization truly successful. As discussed before, there will likely be a high degree of alignment between the leader's personal values and the desired values for the organization.

Personal Values	Current Values	Desired Values
Teamwork	Teamwork	Teamwork
Creativity	Slow decision making	Accountability
Personal growth	Employee development	Continuous improvement
Integrity	Respect	Respect
Financial stability	Cost reduction	Innovation
Accountability	Short-term focus	Profitable growth
Family	Family orientation	Customer satisfaction
Reliability	Adaptability	Fun

Figure 9.3 CEO Chuck's Inquire Results

When reviewing Chuck's assessment in Figure 9.3, we can see his people-focus in personal values such as teamwork, personal growth, and family. He also values stability (financially), accountability, and integrity. Finally, we see a combination of creativity and personal growth that suggests a keen learner.

Chuck's assessment of the current culture shows alignment around respect/integrity, teamwork, family, and employee development. But he also revealed that he thinks the organization has become slower than ideal in its decision making, and he noted the company's short-term focus and energy spent on cost reduction.

In Chuck's view of the desired corporate culture for success, he would like to maintain the family-oriented values of fun, teamwork, accountability, and respect. However, he believes his company needs to grow and mature in terms of its strategic planning, focusing less on cost reduction and more on achieving specific financial targets. He has summed up this preference with the value of achievement orientation. Reflecting on his personal values, he would also like to see creativity and innovation translate to continuous improvement and innovation in the business. Finally, he believes the company needs to start focusing on customer satisfaction.

Step 2: The Leadership Team Assessment

The leadership team also does an assessment to measure the leaders' personal values, their perceptions of the current values in the organization, and the values they believe are required to make the organization successful. The results are consolidated into an overall report and provide a different perspective on the organization.

Personal Values	Current Values	Desired Values
Honesty	Split into silos	Teamwork
Family	Respect	Respect
Responsibility	Results focus	Results focus
Reliability	Best practices	Customer focus
Respect	Adaptability	Achievement orientation
Cooperation	Accountability	Fun
Trust	Internal competition	Empowerment
Friendship	Productivity	Employee recognition

Figure 9.4 Leadership Team Inquire Results

At this stage, the CEO may start to see some disconnect between his perception of the current culture and his leadership team's perception. Indeed, in this case, Chuck notices that while he sees "teams", the people reporting to him see "silos". He has always presented information within the company in terms of the Marketing Team, or the Sales Team, or the Production Team. In fact, he has often offered employee incentives when a specific team meets its targets. In follow-up conversations with his leadership team, he starts to understand that this language and approach has actually created the perception of silos. Yes, there are teams, and within a team there may be teamwork, but in reality, there's very little teamwork across the organization. And the team incentives sometimes cause one team to act in a manner that's detrimental to another team.

Chuck's team defines short-term focus as a best practice. They have always sold cost-cutting requirements to their employees as a way of achieving financial and operating best practices.

The good news is that the leadership team's perception of where the company needs to go is closely aligned with Chuck's. They seem to share many of the same personal values, as well. This alignment bodes well for Chuck. He will not meet a lot of resistance from his leadership team as he starts to implement a shift toward a stronger culture.

Step 3: The Employee Assessment

Samples of employees throughout the organization do the assessment, and the aggregate results are presented to the leadership team. This will be a true test of the connectedness of the leadership team to the day-to-day goings-on of the business.

Personal Values	Current Values	Desired Values
Teamwork	Information hoarding	Transparency
Financial stability	Bureaucracy	Social Responsibility
Reliability	Results focus	Teamwork
Fun	Cost cutting	Fun
Learning	Adaptability	Innovation
Respect	Respect	Respect
Service	Improvement	Accountability
Problem solving	Problem solving	Employee recognition
Family		

Figure 9.5 Employee Inquire Results

Here, the employees' perspective of the organization's current culture takes the contrast between "teamwork" and "silos" one step further to cite the limiting value of information hoarding. They also see slow decision making, but they have identified it as bureaucracy. And while they have also acknowledged cost cutting, they see it through the lens of problem solving and improvement, most likely due to the way the leadership team has presented the concept of best practices.

Figure 9.6 compares the three views of the current culture:

Chuck	Chuck's leadership team	Chuck's employees
Teamwork	Split into silos	Information hoarding
Respect	Respect	Respect
Family oriented	Adaptability	Adaptability
Cost reduction	Best practices	Cost cutting
Short-term focus	Results focus	Results focus
Slow decision making	Accountability	Bureaucracy
Employee development	Internal competition	Problem solving
Adaptability	Productivity	Improvement

Figure 9.6 Current Culture results across three levels in the organization.

When we see the values of the current culture from all three perspectives, we get a glimpse of how the employees view the words and actions of Chuck and his leadership team. When the results were presented to Chuck and his team, they had to agree the employees had reason to see the current culture as they did. There were certainly a few areas that required further clarification. For example, why is Chuck the only one who thinks the current culture includes employee development? What's behind the word bureaucracy? How is information hoarding affecting people's productivity?

Next we get a glimpse into the values that everyone thinks are required to make Chuck's company really successful. Let's compare the three views of the desired culture in Figure 9.7:

Chuck	Chuck's leadership team	Chuck's employees
Customer satisfaction	Customer focus	Corporate social responsibility
Teamwork	Teamwork	Teamwork
Respect	Respect	Respect
Profitable growth	Results focus	Transparency
Fun	Fun	Fun
Innovation	Achievement orientation	Innovation
Accountability	Empowerment	Accountability
Continuous improvement	Employee recognition	Employee recognition

Figure 9.7 Desired Culture results across the organization

When Chuck reviewed these results, he saw there were places where the employees' values aligned well with his—such as teamwork and respect. He also noted that his employees were challenging him to take customer satisfaction and focus to an even higher level, one of corporate social responsibility. He felt encouraged that his leadership team and employees shared his desire to move the company from one of short-term focus and cost cutting to one of innovation and achievement. And clearly there was a desire for more focus on employees and employee recognition.

In this example of Chuck and Chuck's organization, the inquiry was done at various levels within the organization. This is a very basic inquiry. Imagine what else you could learn by introducing other demographic splits. Maybe a view by geographic location would be valuable. Or maybe a function inquiry by department would also provide a valuable perspective. While all this information is valuable, the real value is that it provides the opening to have great discussions with everyone in the organization. As a leader, you may feel nervous to get the results of this inquiry; however, now you have a baseline from which to move forward.

By using modern proven tools that ask the right questions, you've cut right to the heart of the matter. Your culture has been described using the building blocks of culture: *values*. This laser focus will help you find the right answers.

FUEL FOR THOUGHT

🔥 What tools in your life have made things considerably easier?

🔥 Are you ready to embrace and champion a tool to inquire into your organization's culture?

🔥 What demographic inquiries will best serve your organization?

CHAPTER TEN

G is for Gather

In Chapter 9, we saw how using the Culture Transformation Tool allows us to collect valuable data about the culture of our organization. However, as Chip and Dan Heath, the authors of *Made to Stick* have noted, "Data are just summaries of thousands of stories—tell a few of those stories to help make the data meaningful." It's exactly these stories you must seek out during the Gather phase of IGNITE. Without a clear understanding of the words used during the survey inquiry, you can head down the wrong path to shifting your culture. All the effort that you expend will be focused on the wrong goals, and valuable time and credibility will be lost.

Every one of us has different experiences during our lives, and these experiences shape our beliefs and values. As a result, we use words differently to describe events. From my perspective, I may watch my son's hockey game and see a group of 10-year-olds all skating together with matching jerseys. I describe them to my work colleague as a team. However, when the coach of the same group of kids talks to his assistant coach, he has a perspective that they're not a team at all—just a group of 10-year-olds who need to be shaped to perform as a team.

We've both used the word team in our conversations; however, we've used the word with different meanings.

The danger of data is just that. Without the right context, it's easy to place our own interpretation on the meaning of the data. How often have you seen comments on your employee survey asking for more reward and recognition programs? You jump right away to implementing a solution based on your interpretation of what a reward and recognition program should look like. Maybe you introduce a President's Club where the top employees get a valuable prize. You pat yourself on the back for responding to your employees.

The following year, the comment around more reward and recognition comes up again. Now you're frustrated and wonder just how ungrateful your employees can be. You've just awarded 10 52-inch flat screen TVs to your top employees! However, when you take the time to ask a few people why they still think there is a need for reward and recognition programs, you come to understand that rewarding 10 people with TVs was *not* what they were looking for. All they wanted was to be appreciated by their manager and thanked from time to time. By not getting the right context and background to the survey data, you can end up running around in circles.

The first conversation to have is the one about the current culture. There are a number of ways to do this; however in my experience, I find that focus groups are the best way to go. The face-to-face group interaction encourages everyone to tell their story. So much easier than trying to type a long explanation into a box on an online survey! In each group, we discuss the themes that came out of the inquiry phase. For example, in my early days at one particular division at Rogers, a theme emerged around inward focus, blame, and finger pointing. At first, one could make an interpretation that this was all about people not doing their jobs. We asked each employee "how does blame and finger pointing show up in our organization?"

We found out that it actually wasn't about people not being accountable to do their jobs. It was more about the reward and recognition program that we had in place. In order to strive toward operational excellence, our company had put in place a Divisional Race. Points would be awarded to each division based on the achievement of certain metrics. For example, each division focused on reducing the number of customer visits it took to resolve a single service issue. By lowering this metric, we would improve our customer service. Every week the results were published, and each division's position along the race was highlighted to upper management. Unfortunately, my division was usually at the tail end, which was part of the reason I had been brought in—to get them to the front.

By collecting various stories from employees, I gained a better understanding of what drove people to choose words like blame and finger pointing. I also collected a number of ideas about how we could move away from these behaviors. Putting less emphasis on race results and more emphasis on the root causes of the results would generate better results. It wasn't about lack of accountability; everyone was trying very hard to get their job done. The real issues were more about lack of tools, resources, and training. Without delving into the back story, I would never have surfaced these underlying issues.

In another case, one of my clients found the word confusion showing up in their current culture inquiry. This puzzled the leader because he had done a lot of work over the previous 18 months to clarify job descriptions, institute new performance metrics, standardize uniform policies, and restructure some of the departments. If anything, his employees should have more clarity than ever about their jobs! Through the process of gathering feedback about this particular value, he came to understand he was introducing change into the organization at too fast a pace. Employees weren't able to adapt fast enough to everything going on. The information about the changes was flowing through the organization at different speeds, leaving people at different stages of the change. The people in one city were doing things differently than the people in another. And since the employees in both cities often talked to each other, when they found out that each department was doing things differently—well, confusion resulted!

Another theme emerged around integrity, respect, and honesty. These words showed up in the current culture survey, and employees also wanted to preserve them in the desired culture. So we had another good discussion in the focus groups: "Did these words mean the same thing or not?" This theme was an important one for the leader, and he wanted to make sure everyone was on the same page. After hearing from a number of people, he was better equipped to define this value because he had examples of what behavior the employees were describing when they used these words.

Another one of my CEO clients was passionate about the customer experience. He talked about it ALL the time. Whenever there was a conflict with a client, he always asked his employees to find a solution to make the customer happy. It might cost a little bit more money, and it might require an employee to eat some crow, but in the end he believed his business would be better served by serving the customer. His survey showed customer satisfaction as the number-one value in the current culture. Clearly others throughout the organization were receiving his message! Follow-up discussions confirmed that everyone also believed the commitment to the customer was serving the business. They didn't see the customer focus as something valued at their expense. The CEO found these results highly rewarding.

Getting the context for the results in the inquiry phase is critical to moving forward in the right direction. Spending a bit of time here will ensure that you don't take the wrong route forward by placing your own interpretations on the data. It's much better to hear people's perspectives directly than trying to justify the results based on your own personal viewpoints. As your organization gets larger, it's much easier to become disconnected from the front line employees. Your perspective of the organization can become quite different than theirs. You have a different context on the operations than they will have. As a result your actions—while well intentioned like our divisional race—may be interpreted differently than you meant.

By gathering information, you actually accomplish several things. First, you confirm the results of the inquiry phase.

Second, you clarify the context of the values your employees selected. Third, by engaging with your employees, you demonstrate your commitment to the process. You also demonstrate that you value their feedback—that they are important to you. That message will go a long way in getting them to accept the changes bound to come their way as a result of this work. They will feel they were listened to and part of the solution. You'll also gather a list of initiatives or actions that you can take to move the organization forward and use in the Imbed phase of the IGNITE process. Finally, you'll be able to cost out the impact of poor culture. Can you imagine the cost of confusion for that organization that we discussed above? Employees were constantly going back to their managers for clarification!

Opening up the conversations, researching the meaning behind the results, and gathering valuable information from your employees set you up to succeed in the next few phases of the process. Now you have a war chest of stories that can be integrated to produce meaningful actions. There's no second guessing about what people were thinking when they responded to the current culture survey. There's no throwing darts at a dartboard hoping to hit the bull's-eye solution to correct a poor culture. The way forward has been offered up.

FUEL FOR THOUGHT

🔥 Are you willing to invest time and effort in gathering research?

🔥 What resources will you need to help you to gather all the feedback?

🔥 How open will you be to listen to your employees' stories?

CHAPTER ELEVEN

N is for Name

This next phase of IGNITE, the Name phase, is the most common one. Many leaders start their focus on culture here. They begin by naming or calling out the values for their culture. They may declare those values themselves, or it may be part of a leadership activity. Values might even be chosen based on a catalogue of posters with motivational quotes. Either way, starting with naming is a flawed approach because there is no context or connection to the existing organization. However, by following the IGNITE process of Inquire and Gather before Name, the words that you choose to describe the desired culture will be robust and full of meaning for your employees.

Values aren't only used to describe an organizational culture; they are the building blocks of that culture. I like to refer to them as the ingredients of a culture recipe. Naming your ingredients properly will provide clarity to your employees. This is why gathering input about the meaning of certain words used in the inquiry survey is so important. Not only do you need to select these keywords, but you also need to define the behaviors or actions that the words represent. This step ensures employees don't apply their own interpretations to the named values.

When you consider the values required to build a culture that will propel your business forward, you need to remind yourself about where you are. Reflect back to the steps of inquiry and gathering results around your current culture. Use what you've learned to carry forward the positive values that are already part of your success. Add in a few values that will grow your organization, either *away* from current limiting values or *towards* new potential. Your recipe should include three to five values. Each of these values may represent a specific theme you want to emphasize. These are the core values of your organization, the ones most important to driving success for your employees and the business. They must also be authentic values for you personally. If you as the leader cannot "walk the talk," then the exercise will be short-lived.

Once you have chosen these core values, it's critical to define them. Use some of the words from the stories employees told you when asked to explain how specific values show up in the organization. These descriptions will clarify the expected behaviors. People need to understand your expectations in order to carry them out. If you have one definition of accountability and they have another, when it comes time to rating their performance you could be at odds.

This is also a good time to review the vision of the organization. In order to achieve that vision, you need the right culture. Culture is the fuel to reach that vision. If your vision is to be a leader of innovative products, then you will need some sort of reference to creativity or innovation in your core values (think Apple). If your vision is to offer the very best customer experience, then "customer" had better find its way into your core values (think Disney).

Let's go back to Chuck and his leadership team. When Chuck arrived at the Name phase, he gathered his leadership team to discuss the results from the inquiry survey in addition to his own vision for the company's future. The group determined that the five main ingredients for their recipe were teamwork, innovation, achievement orientation, customer focus, and personal growth.

Quantifying the Ingredients

With five ingredients now listed on the fuel recipe card, it was time to actually define each ingredient. Just as "fuel" can mean natural gas, wood, ethanol, petroleum, and so on, each one of us assigns a different meaning to the words used to describe our values. We base that meaning on our own unique experiences and beliefs. Remember, it's critical to clearly define every ingredient with the consensus of the group, so anyone who picks up the recipe will be able to re-create it and pass it on.

This step assembles focus groups from across all levels of the organization to come up with a common definition of each ingredient that resonates with and inspires all employees. A recipe is precise when it comes to the ingredients and the quantity, and the words you use in this step must be just as carefully considered and exact.

Consider these two meanings for "teamwork":

Teamwork—the process of working collaboratively with a group of people to achieve a goal

Teamwork—the fun, family-like, accountable, respectful, and transparent collaboration of everyone across the entire organization to meet the company's long-term strategic goals

Option A represents the current culture in Chuck's organization. Each isolated team works collaboratively to meet that team's incentive. Under Option B, phrases such as "across the entire organization" and "meet the company's goals" emphasize moving beyond isolated teams to collaborate and achieve goals as one larger team. Fun and accountability are integrated within this ingredient in order to provide a sense of balance.

After reviewing all the focus group results, Chuck and his leadership team completed their new fuel recipe. The exercise wasn't easy, and they engaged in much discussion and debate along the way. However, the team came away with much more awareness about the organization's strengths and weaknesses. The team members also learned a lot about what each other found important.

Chuck's Fuel Recipe for the Next 5 Years

Teamwork: *Everyday we contribute to the fun, family-like, accountable, respectful, and transparent collaboration of each of us, across the entire organization, to meet the company's long-term strategic goals.*

Innovation: *We continuously look for ways to innovate and bring in best practices that serve our financial bottom line, our employees, and our customers.*

Achievement Orientation: *We strive to be better each year than the year before, as a company and as individuals. It is equally as important to honor and celebrate our growth as it is to grow.*

Customer Focused: *Without customers, we have no business. We encourage conversations that present the customer view of our products, service, and support.*

Profitable Growth: *Increasing market share through profitable growth will create a long-term, financially stable company with the capability to continue to grow for our employees and customers.*

This phase of the IGNITE process is what moves your culture from one that exists by default to one that thrives by design. By clearly communicating the core values, you will be signaling *how* you expect the work to get done. Employees will be able to assess the organization's values against their own personal values now that your direction is transparent. Those who are aligned to the core values will be motivated to work in this environment. Having clarity on what behaviors are encouraged helps employees make choices on how they react in difficult situations.

Once you have completed your cultural recipe, it's important to communicate it throughout the organization. And yes, having tools for employees to help them refer to and remember the recipe is a benefit. Maybe it's posters, maybe it's desktop reminders, or maybe it's wallet-size cards. All of these accessories are helpful communication devices. However, at the end of the day, success lies in the due diligence that has been done to name those core values. And remember, those names aren't only the names of the values, like teamwork or employee recognition. It's critical to go beyond and name the behaviors that go with the titles of the value. The more specific you are the better. Some leaders even go so far as to give scenarios to their employees so they can see an actual demonstration of the desired behavior. These are the details that employees need because even they aren't really sure what culture is all about. After all, the word "culture" isn't that mainstream.

Inquire, Gather, and Name. This is where all the research and development comes together to create the right fuel for

your specific organization. You haven't borrowed from someone else; it's a personal recipe based on your values, your vision,
and the current state of your organization.

Creating a new fuel recipe is hard work. That's why so many
leaders find it easier just to play with additives. True, time is a
precious commodity in today's business world, but the right
fuel will be more efficient. You may be tempted to reach out
to other leading organizations and copy their core values. If it's
working for Disney, surely it will work for you, right? Don't
be swayed by this shortcut. Every organization is different. The
stage of the business is different, the vision is different, the values of the leaders are different. Doing the work to find the
sludge in the current fuel and determining the right fuel for
your organization's future will move your organization closer to
the launch pad.

FUEL FOR THOUGHT

🔥 What ingredients do you need to add to your
cultural recipe to maximize the fuel?

🔥 What interim steps might you need to take
toward your optimum culture?

🔥 What criteria will you use to select your top three
to five core values?

CHAPTER TWELVE

I is for Imbed

"**A**re we there yet?"

If you're a parent, you're familiar with this phrase. And as a leader, you've probably also experienced it, especially if you've been introducing change into your organization. While moving the organization forward can be rewarding, it also takes a lot of heavy lifting. As you move through your cultural journey, the question "Are we there yet?" will likely come up on several occasions.

This journey started with your commitment to improving your organization's culture. You've brought in the tools to inquire, gathered the research, and named your new values recipe. That was a lot of work. Aren't you there yet? No. This is a common stopping point for many who embark on this journey. However, this simply results in a FAD: Fun And Done.

Now it's time to create the blueprint that will guide you from your current situation to one of competitive advantage. One of the greatest dangers at this point is that you'll create yet another binder of ideas that don't go anywhere. The secret to success is to *build from the blueprint plans*, not store them away for someone else to deal with. Change doesn't happen by creating paper; change happens with action. Rockets don't get to the launch pad unless someone actually builds them. You need a team making tangible efforts. Otherwise all the components remain in the boxes and crates. Beyond all this, you need a complete team engaged to achieve lift-off and move into that space beyond the competition.

It can be relatively easy to collect data, analyze it, and decide where you'd like to go. It takes a blueprint to map out how to get there and how to imbed the changes into your organization. Blueprints can be used to break down the work required to bring your design to life. Architectural blueprints feature many levels. One is an overview of the building that's about to be created. Then there's the floor plan blueprint, an electrical blueprint, an HVAC blueprint, the plumbing blueprint, furniture layouts—and the layers go on and on. The building is constructed based on a defined sequence, with each layer building on the previous work. Specific contractors use specific parts of the blueprint.

The same is true of a cultural blueprint. The overview starts with the goal of achieving the new cultural recipe. The blueprint captures the steps required to get there and the sequencing of the build, and specific tasks are assigned to the appropriate teams. Breaking down the build into achievable tasks allows for action. If tasks are too large, they appear overwhelming, and the builders will find it difficult to get started and maintain momentum. Following the blueprint you create will ensure your organization moves forward.

Chuck's Blueprint

In Chapter 9, we followed Chuck and his leadership team as they conducted assessments to discover their values. In Chapter 11, we observed how they named and defined their culture recipe. While they were excited to share the recipe with the rest of the organization, they realized that to maximize its impact, they needed to back it up with a a sustainable plan. They needed a well-designed rocket ship to accept this powerful fuel recipe. Recall that Chuck's current culture includes values like silos and bureaucracy—things they want to move away from. In addition, they would like to develop values like teamwork and innovation. To do this, the leadership team needs to constantly consider people, processes, and policies. What will need to change to create the desired shift in culture?

Following are the steps that Chuck took next to design his rocket ship:

Step 1 – Imbedding the right people.

Step 2 – Imbedding accountability.

Step 3 – Imbedding innovation.

Let's look at these steps in more detail.

Step 1: Imbedding the right people.

The first step in ensuring your organization grows toward the new culture is to ensure your recruitment and hiring practices support this direction. As Jim Collins stated in his book *Good to Great*, "getting the right people on the bus" is one of the secrets to success.[5] Getting the right people is not only about finding people with the right skills and experience; it's also about finding people who are compatible with your culture. Most of us working in a business have experienced a work colleague who was brilliant but also a pain in the neck.

Zappos is a multibillion-dollar U.S. online sales company known for its customer service and culture. The company has experienced exponential growth since 1999, and its leaders attribute a large portion of this success to their ongoing focus on the organization's culture. Zappos has won many awards as a top business to work for.

In the Zappos organization, the leaders believe so strongly about having the right culture fit, they have a two-tier interview process for potential employees. The first interview focuses on the skills and experience the candidate brings to Zappos. The second interview explores the individual's values and how well the person will fit into the Zappos culture. CEO Tony Hsieh has said he's passed on some brilliant people because they weren't the right match for Zappos. By developing a strong, positive, customer-focused corporate culture, he maintains a competitive advantage.

In tandem, you want to encourage existing employees to move toward and embrace the new culture. Objectives, regular performance assessments, and recognition programs all need to align with the desired values of the organization.

At Chuck's company, the leaders recognized that the way they'd structured their employee objectives and recognition programs actually pitted employees against each other rather than building up teamwork. Their blueprint called for an overhaul of the whole performance-management system. Rather than setting objectives at the individual level, the vice presidents would now set revenue, profit, and new-product objectives for the overall company. The new plan encouraged everyone to work together to achieve the objectives and no longer rewarded the "each man for himself" approach. The cross-functional objectives discouraged the silo effect by requiring different divisions to work together rather than in isolated groups. In addition, the blueprint called for new recognition programs to support the successes of these cross-functional teams. Chuck and his leaders made sure the programs visibly rewarded the change in behavior they desired.

One of the toughest jobs of developing the employee performance blueprint is putting in place a rigorous process to discipline or terminate those employees who won't or can't adjust to the desired culture—the classic situation of having a round peg for a square hole.

For some employees, independent coaching can help them overcome habits that may have been ingrained during years of a different culture. However, other employees may find themselves in an increasingly stressful situation because of the misalignment between their personal values and the corporate culture. These people will find it difficult to adapt.

No one likes to terminate or discipline skilled employees, but the truth is, energy spent working with these individuals would be better spent in a positive manner. And these employees will be much happier and productive when they find an environment that better suits their personal values. If you condone behavior that doesn't fit the new culture, you aren't walking the talk. As the leader, you're required to demonstrate your commitment to the change; you can't simply hang new motivational words on the wall.

Step 2 – Imbedding accountability.

The second step is to prioritize where other changes should be imbedded into the organization. Chuck's employees had suggested a lot of ideas during the gathering phases. However, Chuck believed that moving away from slow decision making and bureaucracy would eliminate a lot of costs and energize his workforce. His team's blueprint called for the creation of an Accountability Task Force that would dig deep into the root causes of bureaucracy and develop a set of recommendations and practices to reduce these wasteful practices. Specifically, it would refocus employees' energy on accountability. Potentially, and most likely, they'd have changes to policy, process, and performance management as an outcome of this activity. These changes would be mapped into future sections of the blueprint. There might even be the need to upgrade or implement new IT systems.

Step 3 – Imbedding innovation.

While the company was currently focused on cost reduction and results, Chuck wanted his employees to change their perspective to one of best practices and innovation. This new focus would still result in cost reductions and better results; however, it would direct people to think about root causes rather than the end game.

So rather than having an objective of cutting departmental costs by 10 percent, the challenge evolved into objectives such as becoming a best-in-class purchasing department. As an employee, wouldn't you rather be working on being best in class rather than nickel and diming everyone to reach your 10 percent cost-reduction target?

That said, when Chuck and his leadership team took into account the amount of change an organization can manage at one time, they decided to postpone the Innovation Task Force program to year two. Overhauling the performance management system and working on bureaucracy was deemed enough for year one.

Chuck and his team continued to map out initiatives and areas of improvement, eventually landing on a three-year plan to move the organization forward.

Chuck's Blueprint Years 1 – 3

Today		Tomorrow
Silos, information hoarding, respect, adaptability, cost reduction, results focus, bureaucracy, problem solving, improvement, short-term focus		Teamwork, innovation, achievement orientation, customer focus, profitable growth
Year 1 - Objectives	**Year 2 – Objectives**	**Year 3 - Objectives**
Objectives, performance-management systems	Continued evolution of the people-management programs	Continued evolution of the people-management programs
New employee recognition programs aligned with objectives and values	Implementation of employee recognition programs	
Development of recruiting and hiring processes	Implement new processes	Review and improve first year of new processes
Coaching programs	Employee assessment against values to ensure development plans are aligned	Review success of coaching programs. Conduct a follow-up values assessment to measure progress
3-year communications plan	Continue execution of communications plan	
Accountability Task Force	Implement recommendations of Accountability Task Force	Continue to implement recommendations
	Innovation Task Force	Implement recommendations of Innovation Task Force

Figure 12.1 Chuck's Year 1–3 Blueprint Overview

Figure 12.1 depicts an overview of part of Chuck's blueprint. Behind this overview, Chuck and his leadership team developed details, including who will do what, project timelines for each initiative, and a governance model to support the blueprint. The governance model is critical to make sure the blueprint doesn't turn into yet another binder of ideas. In fact, Chuck has incorporated the implementation of the blueprint into his leadership team's objectives as part of the accountability value for which they're all striving. These follow-through steps are the tests of walking the talk beyond the initial communication and rollout to the employees.

Like the recipe, the blueprint provides a structure for the leader and the organization. It lists concrete activities that move words into actions. It also provides a visual about who is accountable for the activities and who is affected by them. When everything gets laid out, you can determine if the scope of work is too overwhelming for a particular leader or department. It ensures the cultural shift will take on a life beyond today and not become just another fad. It highlights areas for focus. Leaders can also incorporate such a blueprint into strategy maps, balanced scorecards, or other business management tools.

Every company will have its own unique blueprint based on its situation. Once company leaders map out a blueprint, they're ready for action with a sustainable plan to shift the company's culture. They've calculated the fuel and aligned the design. The captain now has a route mapped out to share with the rest of the crew.

It doesn't matter if someone is driving the rocket, part of the onboard crew, or performing a supporting role on the ground. Everyone is moving toward the same place with the same set of directions. And the sigh of "Are we there yet?" will change to an excited "What's our next destination?"

FUEL FOR THOUGHT

- What filters will you use to prioritize all the ideas and initiatives that can shift your culture?

- How committed is your leadership team to its part of the blueprint?

- How will you keep your blueprint alive as your organization evolves?

CHAPTER THIRTEEN

T is for Track,
E is for Evaluate

Peter Drucker has been quoted as saying "What gets measured gets done." Your cultural journey is very important and deserves no less attention than your revenues, costs, and profits. If you want to truly move your organization and your culture forward, it's essential to have a mechanism in place to measure and monitor the progress. Thus we have arrived at phase number 5 of the IGNITE process, Track. And ultimately you need to check back in with the organization to verify the impact of your initiatives. In Step 6, conducting an Evaluation of the effectiveness of your initiatives is just as important as getting them done.

Some organizations, especially those that are run by entrepreneurs, are less disciplined on the reporting front. Others are very sophisticated using strategy maps, balanced scorecards, and dashboards. You can report on your cultural initiatives separately, or you can integrate them into existing reports. Either way, the important thing to remember is you must be able to assign accountability for action and measure the degree of action. Tracking brings action into focus. It's where the fuel becomes active. It ensures that lift-off actually occurs.

In the previous chapter, we covered creating a blueprint for action in order to imbed culture changes. This blueprint is an excellent tool to use to develop your tracking system. Sometimes, you will be able to attribute direct results. Perhaps you will set targets like a 10 percent reduction in employee turnover or a 3 percent increase in customer satisfaction. Other goals may be more project-oriented, where you will need to monitor achievement of milestones as the project progresses. A good project-management software program can provide high-level reports that will help your leadership team keep track of what's going on.

Managers are asked to write many reports. The reports that you ask them to focus on will drive their priorities. Improving your culture drives so many benefits, don't let it get lost in the shuffle of financial reporting. Unless of course, you're reporting on the financial benefits of addressing limiting values!

Tracking progress not only helps on the accountability front, it also helps identify when it might be time to adjust an activity. External circumstances may be impacting your business, or an internal crisis may have occurred. Recalibration is as much a part of the tracking activity as is the actual reporting on progress.

Implementing initiatives to shift culture are not overnight activities. For example, you don't throw the switch and suddenly expect bureaucracy to disappear. Tracking initiatives to reduce bureaucracy is part of the equation.

In his blueprint, Chuck had identified a number of items for his Human Resources department. This included the creation of a hiring tool that would incorporate a values assessment of the candidate. He also asked that the performance-management system be adjusted to reflect not only "what" employees were accomplishing but also "how." Finally, they had to raise the bar on employee recognition. The team got together and discussed what metrics they could use to help them measure their success during the year. In some cases, it would be their ability to hit project milestones; in other cases it would be specific results.

Anne was tasked with overseeing an improved performance-management system. She knew it would involve these key milestones:

- Updating the performance-management tool to include a section on values
- Training for all managers on how to use the new tool
- Communication to all employees on the new performance-management criteria and how it would be applied
- Implementation of the new tool for the year-end performance-management process

Anne decided that this initiative would be successful if she could have the tool updated in the first quarter. The second quarter would be a good time for the communication and training. The end target would be 100-percent adoption of the new tool during the year-end performance-management cycle. Recognizing the organization's shift in values and new emphasis on *how* work got done, Anne also recommended that this section of the performance evaluation would hold less impact as it was rolled out the first year. After all, if employees didn't know how and on what they were going to be measured until mid-year, was it really fair? Anne also had to be sensitive to the financial implications of the program, so she was going to need some financial indicators to measure her success. In this case, the company couldn't afford to invest $1 million on a new performance-management tool. She would need to stay within the boundaries of the budgets allocated to her.

For Anne, setting up a focused scorecard that took into consideration all aspects for her initiative, not just the financial aspect, helped her to meet her objectives for that first year. Focusing solely on her budgets wouldn't ensure she met project timelines. Focusing on her project timelines wouldn't ensure she met her budgets. She had to have a balanced scorecard that looked across the initiative.

Other managers in Chuck's organization set up scorecards, and all of those rolled up into a master scorecard for Chuck. There were ebbs and flows in the organization's progress, but progress was being made.

And once a reasonable length of time has gone by, you also need to measure the effectiveness of the initiatives. This is where Step 6 of the IGNITE process, Evaluate, comes into play. You can best measure the effectiveness of the initiatives by *evaluating* the culture again. Using the same inquiry assessment tools you used before allows you to monitor the progress against the baseline you created with the initial survey. After 18 months, Chuck decided it was time to check in with his employees. He ran the inquiry assessment tool and was pleased to see that information hoarding had disappeared from the description of the current culture. It signaled that positive change was occurring.

Too often, we get caught up in the running the day-to-day activities of our business. However, if we're committed to the cultural journey then we must also be committed to tracking the results just as diligently as we track our usual financial results. Unless we have something to review, we can't be confident that we're staying accountable to progress. Unless we see indications of missed milestones, we can't react to the issues until it's too late.

And of course everything has to be in context of what's going on around us. Sometimes the most important role that reporting can play is to identify trends. If one particular department is consistently missing targets, then maybe that team has too much on its plate and recalibration needs to take place. Or perhaps the company hasn't identified enough resources to match the level of work assigned. Tracking is like the canary in the coal mine. It not only provides us with a picture of what's been achieved; it can also act as a predictor of the future. If your culture initiatives are all falling by the wayside, it's unreasonable to expect you'll see change when you do your evaluation.

Tracking and evaluating ensures the success of imbedding your initiatives. If you can't imbed changes in your organization, then you've ended up on the FAD side of things. All the work done to inquire, gather, and name will be for naught. All the work done to identify initiatives to shift your culture will have been wasted. And in the meantime, all the advantages your company can gain from a strong positive culture will be lost.

Tracking and evaluating are no strangers to our organizations. Applying them to culture may be new, but it's not foreign. By employing standard reporting techniques like project reporting, your culture initiatives can be just as easily incorporated into standard reporting packages. And you've already used the assessment tool, so running the evaluation is just a repeat performance. The biggest benefit of tracking is that it lifts initiatives off the paper. It causes them to be real. Inquire, Gather, Name, Imbed, Track and Evaluate. IGNITE. It's what moves your rocket ship past the launch pad.

FUEL FOR THOUGHT

How can you ensure the progress of your cultural journey through measurement?

How will you give your cultural journey the priority it needs when it comes to reporting organizational results?

Have you set a target for evaluating the success of your blueprint?

CHAPTER FOURTEEN

"Why Don't They Do What I Say?"

As leaders in our organizations, we often become frustrated when we see a vision so clearly in our minds, yet our employees just don't seem to get it. Over and over, they question us and resist the changes we try to implement. When this happens, any forward movement slows to a snail's pace.

This phenomenon is perhaps even more prevalent when we try to shift underlying culture because this involves changing beliefs and behaviors. Let's look at an historic example. In 1961, John F. Kennedy declared that the United States should set a goal to land a man on the moon before the end of the decade. The USSR had raised the competitive bar during the 1950s, becoming a leader in space programs and research. The launch of Sputnik in 1957 exposed gaps in American technology. For the United States, creating a rocket capable of putting a man on the moon was an ambitious goal—one that required a change in focus, resources, and manpower. It also required a change in the behaviors of those needed to support the program. In the following excerpt from JFK's speech, he asked people to embrace a new blueprint to build a rocket ship capable of putting a man on the moon and to incorporate a recipe of values to fuel this initiative.

This decision demands a major national commitment of scientific and technical manpower, materiel [sic] and facilities, and the possibility of their diversion from other important activities where they are already thinly spread. It means a degree of dedication, organization and discipline which have not always characterized our research and development efforts. It means we cannot afford undue work stoppages, inflated costs of material or talent, wasteful interagency rivalries, or a high turnover of key personnel.

New objectives and new money cannot solve these problems. They could in fact, aggravate them further—unless every scientist, every engineer, every serviceman, every technician, contractor, and civil servant gives his personal pledge that this nation will move forward, with the full speed of freedom, in the exciting adventure of space.[6]

Too often, we believe the work has been done once the plans have been created, documented, and communicated. Sometimes we even go so far as to set objectives and metrics to help us measure the progress of the plan's implementation. We can change the policies, processes, and even the systems. But moving *people* to change—the very people we need to make the organization run—is a skill all its own. And it's not easy!

When most people think of leaders, they talk about their ability to lead people through difficult times, through an organization's evolution, or through new and ongoing challenges. What skill are these leaders really practicing? Exceptional change management.

Change Management

As a formal discipline, change management hasn't been around long. Kurt Lewin, a Gestalt social psychologist, has been acknowledged as the "father of social change theories" since he started writing on this topic in the late 1930s.

However, it really wasn't until the 1990s that work in this area became prevalent and the phrase "change management" started to appear. The tipping point came in 1996 with the publication of John Kotter's *Leading Change*, which outlines an eight-step process for implementing successful transformations. (It became the number-one management book of the year.) Not until 2011 was the Association of Change Management Professionals established. So we can be excused if we're not all experts in this relatively new and emerging field.

Yet without our changes formally integrated into our organizations, we'll find ourselves at year's end once again staring at those dusty binders, those stagnant metrics, and the confused faces of our employees. Successfully moving the bar on your culture requires conducting a vibrant change-management process.

I'm almost embarrassed to talk about my first exposure to change management. We were trying to implement a new information-management system. The vendor warned us over and over that without a proper change-management plan, the likelihood of successful implementation would be low. Heeding those words, we called on our HR team to help us. Early on in the project, we set up workshops with the implementation team to talk about change, how we react to change, and what kind of support we needed to make the required changes. We did all the right things, role playing situations involving change and talking about our fear of change. We were on it!

In selling the need to introduce this new system, we presented the business case around the management table. We also worked the back rooms to eliminate naysayers, and we pushed our leader to discuss the need for the capital budget with the CFO. It was a tough communication job to make this sale; however, we convinced people it was the right path forward. The sense of urgency we created encouraged people to accept the need for the change.

Our job was done. We had the team on board with respect to the value of the implementation and the roles they were required to play. We had the leadership team's commitment to the project and approval of the funds. So we marched ahead with the project. Several months later, we were ready to do a pilot. The implementation was a bit bumpy to start, but that's the point of doing a pilot, after all. We needed to tweak some of the IT configurations, clarify a few of our training documents and identify extra support. We smoothed them out and moved on to our first small but authentic implementation.

Once again, we hit a few bumps. But we had chosen a small market for our launch, so any issues would affect fewer than 5 percent of our customers. Again we smoothed out the bumps in the software, and we moved on to a medium-sized market (approximately 20 percent of our customer base). Then things ground to a halt. It seemed not a single person would try to use the new system. The hue and cry over the system's failures became louder than honking taxi cabs in New York City.

So we put employees through more training, had early morning team huddles, and added resources to help us through the learning curves where productivity often dips. Months went by, and we still couldn't seem to get anyone to embrace the new system. We met with resistance everywhere. The implementation team's credibility was shot, and the negative feedback that made its way up to the leadership team prompted them to question the investment.

Finally, after much work and heavy lifting, the system was fully implemented. And yes, it's achieved many of the promised benefits. But surely there was a better, more efficient, less costly way to do it.

Later, at a conference hosted by the Association of Change Management Professionals, I learned via a 2008 IBM study titled *Making Change Work* that 40 percent of projects fail to meet at least one of their objectives. In addition, a full 15 percent either stopped or failed to meet *any* of their objectives. At the same conference, I became aware of the world leader in research and content creation in the field of change management, Prosci. I learned about Prosci's work to formalize the discipline of change management, as well as tools to help organizations move through change.

ADKAR – A Tool for Change

One of those tools is the change-management curve model. Foundational to change management, this model describes the five stages an organization must complete to successfully implement change: **Awareness, Desire, Knowledge, Ability, and Reinforcement.** Also known as the ADKAR model, this results-oriented change-management model was developed by Jeff Hiatt in 1995 and later published in a 1998 article titled "The Perfect Change" by the Change Management Learning Center.

Awareness
Desire
Knowledge
Ability
Reinforcement®

Figure 14.1: The ADKAR model[7]

Whether your journey is software implementation or a shift in culture, you can't just stand up, announce change, and expect overnight results. Even when you produce a roadmap or a blueprint for your employees to follow, you need to motivate them to want to read the plan—and motivate them even more to change their beliefs and behaviors. As a leader, you need to embrace the work required. Setting up a formal change-management process within your organization is the first step.

Stage 1 – Awareness. The journey to shift culture starts with the awareness stage. Management communicates that the company is undertaking the journey and asks employees to participate in surveys, feedback forums, and focus groups. But if managers don't explain the why, providing context for the journey, they'll find that many employees resist even at this early stage. To take an example outside the business world, picture a four-year-old child, brown eyes gazing up at you, curiously asking you "why?" after every phrase you utter. Or the steely blue eyes of your teenager staring back at you, challenging every request you make. Well, it turns out that getting older doesn't diminish our need to understand *why* we're being asked to change. As leaders, we must communicate the why over and over again—along with who, what, when, where, and how.

The awareness stage is the time to explain to employees the importance of good culture to company success. It's the time to communicate the process your organization will follow to discover the current culture, identify the needed culture, build the recipe and the blueprint, and engage employees in improving the culture.

Stage 2 – Desire. The desire stage is all about answering the question "What's in it for me?" While managers often find it virtually impossible to dictate change to an employee, they can take certain steps to help employees *choose* to change. The first is to be a good listener and empathize with an employee's concerns. For example, have employees identify barriers that make it difficult for them to accept the change. It can also help to focus on *what* will change rather than *how* the change will be made. Once employees understand what will change, they may volunteer ways to make the change happen—and that, in turn, will make the change more palatable and acceptable to them.

Demonstrating the benefits of change can also be helpful. Seeing is believing: Share case studies from other companies that have transformed their culture, bring in people who have successfully made the shift to an improved culture, or take a field trip to a company that has the type of culture you're trying to create.

Stage 3 – Knowledge. After awareness and desire comes knowledge. Here, employees need to know both *what* to change and *how* to change. If your culture shift includes a change in systems or processes, knowledge of the change and how to change can be managed through training and education programs. Suppose you aim to reduce bureaucracy by implementing a new automated system. Providing awareness of the new system and its benefits to your employees will help them more readily embrace the training. If you make a shift that involves changing behavior, then you may find individual coaching and mentoring will help employees through the change. After all, employees don't become team players overnight just because you've decreed it! They need knowledge about what teamwork is, what it looks like, and how you expect teams to play together. It's like learning to play tennis. First you need someone to explain what a forehand shot is and show you what it looks like. Then you have a chance of hitting the ball.

Stage 4 – Ability. Even with all the knowledge in the world, the ability to translate knowledge into practice can be a challenge. People learn at different rates, so the ability to enact changes may differ from employee to employee. Habits are difficult to break. Again, individual coaching and mentoring can be helpful to show employees how to move from knowledge to action.

Stage 5 – Reinforcement. The final step to making a real change is reinforcement. Having a coach nearby as you practice your forehand shot helps you improve your ability to hit the ball. Getting feedback and a high-five when they do things right motivates and inspires people to do more.

The larger the changes you're seeking, the more critical employee support becomes. In one instance, we wanted to improve employee recognition in our culture. To support this goal, the management team decided we would simply personally thank our employees more often. We knew, based on feedback from our employees, that if we followed through, they would feel better recognized. We also knew we could communicate thanks in person, by email, or by voice mail. Now we had to act on what we knew to reinforce the behavior we wanted.

In order to make sure we actually changed our behaviors, we set a target of three thank-you messages a week each, and then we reported our progress to each other. In this manner, we developed a support system as we practiced the new behavior. If someone struggled, we'd suggest where they could find opportunities to say thank you. If someone made only two thank-you's in the first few weeks, we'd help them by asking them to share the results of those two thank-you's. When they took the time to reflect on how their expressions of gratitude affected employees, they became more motivated to keep trying.

Making a shift in your organization's culture is a daunting task. However, applying the methods described here is key to making your strategies come alive. Don't let all your hard work at the front end turn into a dusty binder full of "what could have been." Anticipate that your Culture Blueprint will be filled with changes, and complement your work with a change-management program. Helping your employees embrace change will improve your chances of success. You won't become just another statistic in IBM's study of failed projects. Instead, you'll further ensure positive long-term results.

FUEL FOR THOUGHT

🔥 Do you have a clear understanding of change management?

🔥 What do you need to do to formalize change management within your organization?

🔥 Where can you best use change management to ensure the success of your culture change?

CHAPTER FIFTEEN

Generational Culture

Today in my business, I look around and realize my colleagues could be my father, my daughter, and my grandson. My daughter's friend Dan works with colleagues who could be his great-grandfather, his grandmother, and his uncle. Research done in 2007 shows an important shift: a workplace mostly defined by three generations in 1977 is being defined by four in 2013.

Nine out of 10 workplaces in Canada currently employ four generations, requiring leaders to grasp the implications of this new reality. Your perspective will depend on where you fall on the generational timeline, but as a leader in your organization, you need to understand how each generation's values and beliefs influence your corporate culture. In fact, how you manage and communicate with each generation will define your ability to motivate your employees, knowing that incorporating their personal values into your corporate culture will fuel their productivity.

Each generation has developed its own set of values based on its unique experiences of the world. While I can generalize about each generation, it's helpful to apply some of that information specifically in the context in today's workplaces. After all, four generations in the workplace create a spectrum of personal values that's broader than ever before. So what do these four generations look like?

Naming the Generations

First, let's look at the current variety of generations and name them:

- **Traditionalists**, also known as the Silent Generation or the Great Generation, were born between 1922 and 1945.
- **Baby Boomers** were born between 1946 and 1964.
- **Generation X** was born between 1965 and 1980.
- **Generation Y,** or the Millennials, were born between 1981 and 1991.

You can pick out *your* generation easily, but how about the rest of your organization? How much does each generation influence your company?

To a great degree, the Traditionalist generation has moved out of the workplace, and the Baby Boomers are in the process of retiring. Generations X and Y are filling those slots. However, in sheer numbers, Generation Y is the largest generation since the Baby Boomers, making Generation X the "sandwich" generation in the workplace. By 2015, Generation Y will outnumber Generation X in the workplace by two to one!

The U.S. Bureau of Labor Statistics has been tracking the flow of these generations through our workplace. This has also enabled them to predict what our organizations will look like going out to 2020. By then, a fifth generation—Gen2020—will be entering the workplace. Figure 15.1 highlights how organizations will be overtaken by Generation Y.

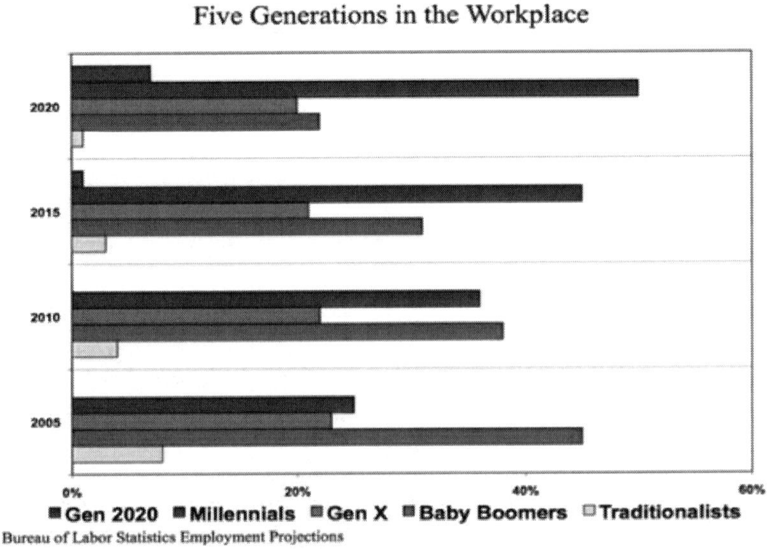

Five Generations in the Workplace

Bureau of Labor Statistics Employment Projections

Figure 15.1 Generations in the Workplace

Meet Robert, Mark, Donna, and Matt

Our personal values are influenced by our own experiences and personal beliefs. Landmark events specific to each generation helped shape that generation's value system.

Robert is a Traditionalist. The only son of William and Rose, he was born in 1943, not long after the end of the Great Depression, which stretched from 1929 to 1933. His childhood was one of scarcity and penny pinching, and he entered the workplace with the attitude that work was all about supporting his family. Highly loyal, he spent almost four decades with the same employer. Robert believes that people get ahead through hard work and "earning their stripes." For example, all summer students have to pass the hiring tests of the organization, even if they're relatives of employees. No free passes just because your aunt is a vice president! Robert has spent most of his life without computers and the instant communications that come with today's cell phones. He prefers the personal touch and meeting with people one-on-one. For this reason, he embraces the technology of Skype over texting because Skype video conversations allow him more personal interaction.

Mark is a Baby Boomer, born in 1956. He grew up with a Traditionalist father and mother, who believed everything must be earned. His parents paid out his weekly allowance only if he completed all his chores, and half the money had to go toward a savings account.

As a teenager and young adult, Mark started to question the authority figures in his life. He grew his hair long and turned up the rock-and-roll music until the house shook. It was an era to effect change—from putting a man on the moon, to organizing against the Vietnam War and raising awareness about environmental issues such as DDT and acid rain. To gain more financial freedom, Mark worked long hours, becoming one of the many individuals who created the standard 60-hour work week. Putting in these hours meant he could afford a new car and a house in the suburbs. For Mark, "face time" at the office translates to "hard work," and he expects to be rewarded and recognized for this dedication.

Donna, born in 1973, belongs to Generation X. Donna grew up in an era of women entering the workplace, so both her parents worked. And while this presented a two-income family with additional financial flexibility, it also meant that some of those dollars were spent on Donna's day care. Donna became self-sufficient and resourceful at an early age.

When she was a teenager, her parents divorced. Her father has been laid off from several positions over the years, and his pension is in jeopardy. These personal experiences, along with events such as the Enron scandal and the dot-com bust, have made Donna distrustful of leaders. Because she's so independent, she dislikes being micro-managed and has changed employers three times already to get ahead.

As an adult, Donna now seeks flex-time and work-life balance so she can spend more time with her husband and kids. Family is important to her. She works to live, not the other way around. And she enjoys the tools of "instant gratification" that have become part of her everyday life: ATMs, microwave ovens, remote controls, and the Internet.

And finally, meet Matt. Born in 1990, he is just entering the workforce—maybe. As he likes to tell his mom and dad, "Live, then work!" Matt has been plugged in since the day he was born. A typical day may include Nintendo, chat programs, Face-Time via his iPhone, and downloading music from the Internet. Why do one thing at a time when you can multitask?

Matt grew up with the Nike slogan "Just Do It!" He played

hockey, soccer, and baseball, collecting trophies for every-thing from a championship to most improved. However, Matt is very laid back, casual, and informal. He knows most of his high school teachers on a first-name basis. Now that Matt has graduated from college, he's interviewing a number of potential employers to find the right boss and a role where he can make a difference. He bubbles over with lots of ideas that he wants to put into action—an entrepreneurial attitude. And he expects to step in and take on a leadership role from the get-go.

Cheryl Cran is the author of *101 Ways to Make Generations X, Y, and Zoomers Happy at Work*. In Figure 15.2, she has summarized a number of the workplace characteristics for each generation.

Generations In the Workplace	Work Values	Work is Defined as...	Life Values	Work & Family
Traditionalists In their late 60's and older	Hard and labor intensive Follow rules, hierarchical	Have to do it to support the family	Commitment Frugality Comfortable	Family was second to work
Zoomers Early 50's to late 60's	Authority rules, rules are needed, work hard and then retire	A way to build success and monetary gain for self and family	Freedom Work role is identity Retirement is a goal	Family knew that parents had to work hard to create lifestyle
Gen X 30's to early 50's	Replace task with technology, projects are better than tasks	Necessary yet not primary, work needs to be balanced with family	Family balance Flexible Technology for getting things done	Want to work from home to increase family time
Gen Y 20's to early 30's	Focused on learning and growth, fast recognition, looking for career path	Does not define, is a part time focus, is not long term in one job	Life is before work Fun in all things Technology for connection	Family and friends first Time off for family and friends

Figure 15.2 Generational Workplace Characteristics[8]

So what happens when we bring these generations together in the workplace? I experienced the cultural divide firsthand when I was recruiting for a new work function. Yes, I'm that Baby Boomer boss—and young, recently graduated MBAs applied for the position. I went through my normal interview process, seeking to understand their skills, experience, and motivations. When I've interviewed Baby Boomers, they've often had difficulty answering questions about motivations. Generation Y interviewees, on the other hand, discussed their motivations enthusiastically.

More important, these candidates wanted to make sure that the environment of the hiring department matched their desired environment. They were quick to take over the interviewing at this stage, peppering me with questions about my management style, how soon they could progress into a new position, what technology would be made available to them, how much exposure they would have to senior management, whether they could work flexible hours, and so on.

It often bothered me to hear these young people demand instant access to benefits that had taken me years to acquire. In one case, a college intern was granted a management position— at only 21, for crying out loud! But he was smart and energetic, so the department hired him. And once on the payroll, he kept pushing, wanting to upgrade and acquire new computer equipment, as well as install programs the rest of us had never heard of to improve his efficiency and effectiveness.

Yet with that exposure, our department started to embrace new ways of doing things. Instead of running up long-distance bills with traditional national conference calls, we embraced Skype. And then, true to form for Generation Y, the young manager left after two and a half years to seek his next adventure.

Same Goal, Different Play

Bill, Mark, Donna, and Matt work in the same office. While they're all trying to achieve the same goals, they will take different paths to get there. Companies that embrace these generational differences have found a way to include generational diversity as part of their competitive advantage.

When it comes to corporate culture, it's important to understand the influence of each generation. Labor shortages and the decline of a mandatory retirement age have resulted in Baby Boomers staying in the workplace longer. Right now, Baby Boomers still hold most managerial and leadership positions, and as such, their values and actions dictate the culture of their organizations. In the meantime, Generation X and Generation Y are pushing their way into the workforce, making up more than 50 percent of the employee base. By 2020, as Generation X moves into leadership positions, Generation Y will make up 50 percent of the workforce.

When you do your culture assessments, the impact of these generational waves and their personal value systems will influence the desired culture. Because of each generation's unique perspective, each will also assign different meaning to certain values. This makes a group discussion and definition of each recipe ingredient that much more important.

Differing Definitions of Feedback

For example, the value of "open communication" is most sought-after across all generations. But for Traditionalists and Baby Boomers, this concept means presenting and sharing information. It doesn't include feedback. For them, feedback is often seen as criticism. They adhere to the "if you don't hear from me, you're doing fine" style of communication.

At the other end of the spectrum, Generation Y demands lots of communication—not necessarily face to face but ongoing. For them, open communication is about learning and improvement. Feedback is a critical part of this communication, and they want lots of it. If open communication is a key value in your values recipe, what support will you need to create for your Baby Boomers to help them understand this new definition of open communication?

Looking to the Future of Your Culture

If Baby Boomer leaders continue to push their values without taking into consideration the values of Generations X and Y, they could find themselves at a competitive disadvantage when hiring and retaining talent. Defining the culture is an important first step; however, adjusting policies and processes to create the desired culture is what separates one company from another in the end.

The leaders who also take into account the different generational value systems as part of the corporate culture strategy are wisely taking issues to the next level. Your culture "succession" plan is as critical to your organization's success as your leadership succession plan. Ten years from now, when more members of Generation X hold managerial and leadership positions and the volume of Generation Y workers has doubled, how will your organization's culture need to evolve to meet their needs? If you have poor culture now and don't start down the path to improve it, you may find yourself in a corporate culture crisis later. You may not be one of the top employers to work for, but can you afford to be one of the worst?

The demand for a flexible work life is going to increase. First, as companies become more global, employees are facing multiple time zones when trying to get work done. The traditional 9 to 5 work day no longer fits when working with people halfway around the world.

Second, technology provides the ability to work anytime anywhere. And Generation Yers have grown up on technology. They can be much more productive working from home or a satellite office rather than stuck in traffic for hours each day. Today, it's more about the output and less about the face time.

In response to this demand for flexibility, more and more organizations are remunerating their employees based on pay for performance. For example, in 2004, Best Buy implemented a Results Only Work Environment (ROWE) focusing on performance and less on office attendance. The flexible working condition demand is already on the rise. According to a study produced by the Society for Human Resource Management and the Families and Work Institute in 2012, 63 percent of companies allowed employees to work some hours from home, compared with 34 percent in 2005.

Our organizational cultures need to adapt to this new working environment. Processes and policies that worked when everyone had a solitary cubicle on the same floor just aren't as relevant in a dynamic workplace.

Keeping employees engaged will be even more challenging, with Generation Y employees expected to move every two to three years. How much will you be willing to invest in hiring and training if your new employees will give you such a short commitment? You'll need to provide incentives for them to hang around a while. Appealing to the things that matter most for this generation is the way to go. Lots of on-going coaching and feedback, the opportunity to try something new and challenging through rotating job assignments, or enhancing their sense of team and community are job aspects they will appreciate. Shifting your culture to embrace coaching, changing accountabilities, and community requires a current inventory of these skills and abilities.

Keeping up with technology will also push organizations. Generations X and Y have grown up with the Internet and every advancing technology. The latest technology is part of their personal lives, and they won't put up with archaic communication systems or not having the latest tools to help with their work. People are already using their personal iPads for added mobility and features, leaving their corporate laptops in the office. These are just three examples of how your organization's design will have to adapt in order to keep the culture in sync with today's employees.

Remember that Generation Ys are now researching and

interviewing companies based on their corporate cultures. You can't just put the right buzz words up on posters and the corporate website. Those in Generations X and Y come with a built-in mistrust of leadership, and they will see through that "game" faster than anyone. And because they're so socially connected, with thousands of followers, it won't take long to get the word out about their organization's culture—the good and the bad!

So whether you're a Bill, Mark, Donna, or Matt, remember that each generation contributes to the corporate culture and has needs within that culture.

FUEL FOR THOUGHT

🔥 Do you know the generational makeup of your organization?

🔥 What impact does this have on the culture of your organization?

🔥 What shifts in your organizational culture do you need to consider now in order to hire the best talent from Generation Y?

CHAPTER SIXTEEN

Culture from the Management Trenches

"Transformation of the organization begins with the personal transformation of the leadership," says Richard Barrett, founder and chairman of the Barrett Values Center.

That's great—if you happen to be working in a company with great leadership, or on an enlightened leadership team actively engaged in managing the organization's culture.

However, what if you're down in the middle-management trenches with a strong desire to help shift the organization but little or no support from the top? I hear this complaint repeatedly from both front-line and middle managers.

Can culture change from the bottom up?

When we look around the globe, we can see several examples of organizational culture changing from the bottom up. However, in most cases, this has played out in a revolutionary style, as witnessed in Egypt with President Hosni Mubarak and in Libya with President Muammar Gaddafi. When the citizens in a nation rise up and demand a change in government, they're also pleading for a change in organizational culture.

They no longer wish to live in a world of corrupt leaders bent on self-interest only. And with ever-increasing ways to mobilize the "discontented" using social media and wireless technology, the power to effect change can shift into the hands of the persecuted. Egypt and Libya are extreme cases of changing culture from the bottom up, yet they happen!

Change from Down in the Corporate Trenches

The opportunity to change culture from the trenches also exists within large companies. Because a large company can be described as a collection of medium-sized businesses, an organization's culture can in fact differ within its various divisions. The leaders of these medium-sized groups set the tone for a culture of their own, especially when top leaders don't provide clear direction or send conflicting messages.

Even within medium-sized companies, the culture within each function can vary. For example, the sales people in an organization get so focused on customer relationships, they appear to operate with a culture of customer first followed by fun and community involvement. In contrast, those in the finance and administrative functions focus on cost reduction, continuous opportunity, and employee development.

Clearly, opportunities do exist for managers to influence the culture of the people directly around them. And while it's rarely good to pull your troops out of the line that the company's "general" has set, managers can still choose *how* to move along that line to achieve the desired goals of the company.

Headquarters: The Center of the Earth

Like many other middle managers, I struggled in the trenches of the workplace. Specifically, I was leading an operations team for Rogers Communications in Ottawa, a newly acquired division within the large Toronto-based company. A significant amount of centralization had occurred in the previous two years, leaving the perception that everything happens in Toronto.

In particular, external communications and media events always centered around Headquarters—the center of the Earth. That left employees in Ottawa feeling like second-class citizens. Besides, those in the Toronto operations group always seemed better informed than those of us in the outer regions. As a result, we had been lulled into believing the generals at Headquarters inevitably directed our destiny. That meant we'd be told if, when, and how to march ahead.

So we sat back and waited for Headquarters to come out with the grand declaration of our company's mission, vision, and values. We knew an old vision statement was collecting dust somewhere in the company's archives. But with vision, mission, and values being the hot business topics of the day, surely *someone* down in Headquarters was working on this trinity, right?

Month after month of lack of direction from Headquarters led to increasing frustration. Yet sometimes, it just takes one shift in perspective to change things. So I decided instead of considering myself as a middle-management captain in the overall organization, I needed to see myself as the *general*—the commander in charge—of the region.

Trying on this new perspective, I took responsibility to change our culture from my position down in the trenches. This decision also initiated a personal transformation.

Two-Day Meeting Set Foundation for Change

I began by laying critical groundwork, something that put all team members on the same page. Some were relatively new to the company; others had been there a long time. As a working team, we didn't know each other well, and we certainly didn't understand the priorities Headquarters intended for each area within our division.

So we conducted a two-day offsite meeting to pull our group together. We calibrated our knowledge of the internal and external factors we worked within. We brought in experts from inside and outside our organization to share *their* visions of our company, our industry, and the eastern Ontario region. Armed with this foundational information, we built a vision and purpose for ourselves.

Our purpose: Making people's lives in Ottawa easier and more enjoyable through world-class service and leading-edge technology.

Our vision: Rogers Ottawa will be the most trusted and respected "go to" company for all communication solutions in Ottawa, with world-class operational and people practices.

The bonus? Neither one of these statements would take us off the course that Headquarters had us on (even if one had been explicitly charted).

Then we began a conversation about how we'd work together—and how we *needed* to work together to live our purpose and vision. We learned about our different personality and communication styles, what made us unique, and what we had in common. We shared our personal values. In fact, we created our own values recipe and coached each other to behave within these values. Accountability, fun, and integrity—the values deemed important to all of us—became part of that recipe. This made it easy to coach each other with humor and respect.

As we coalesced around the values we'd identified as important, the team's energy levels started to build. Taking control and empowering ourselves to lead our own troops in our chosen manner excited us! And so, having taken the initiative to create our own positive culture and experience firsthand how this made our work more productive and purposeful, we took on a second challenge. We identified the things we didn't like about the way Headquarters treated us and shifted them around to take ownership and act differently. Rather than be victims of circumstance, we became creators of our destiny.

Journey to Accountability

And so the journey began. We stopped blaming Headquarters for things, and we took accountability to change the way we were being treated by Headquarters. For example, we'd decided communication was one item we felt passionate about. To be more effective, we needed to have open communications. This change was easy enough within our own team, but we also needed to take ownership to create the communications we needed from Headquarters. If we felt that someone from Headquarters wasn't communicating enough with us, we invited that person to present at our meetings. We no longer sat around complaining about the lack of communication from above; we created opportunities for communication from below.

Due to our efforts to shift perspective and create a more positive culture, our results continued to progress over the next few years. Not only did we improve our financial and key operational indicators, but other departments within Rogers reached out and wanted to become involved with us. Over and over again, we heard phrases like "you folks in Ottawa are just such a pleasure to do business with," or "Carol, your team is always ready to step up to help find solutions. It's so refreshing."

Remember, in this case we stepped into our own leadership role. We discovered we didn't need to be at the pinnacle of a large organization to make these types of changes; we could do it from any level. Too often, we wait for somebody to come along and teach us what to do. Or we wait for somebody to arrive and take control. Or we wait for somebody else to pick up the pieces.

How many times have you taken this approach? Do you remember the last time you walked past an almost disintegrated piece of newspaper flapping under the bush at the end of your driveway? Did you leave it for somebody else to pick up? Isn't it time to be your own somebody?

As it turned out, when I finally chose to change the culture from the trenches, the timing couldn't have been better. From the late 1990s to the mid-2000s, Rogers went through a number of CEOs at the Cable division. Colin Watson, Jos Wintermans, Trey Smith, and John Tory. Ted Rogers himself even took on the role during the transitions in management.

Each CEO came with his own vision, values, management style, and impact on culture. For example, in her book *High Wire Act*, Caroline Van Hasselt describes Jos Wintermans's 11-month tenure as one in which he "cleaned house, eliminated dead wood, simplified the organizational structure and restructured the capital budget. He reduced the number of vice presidents reporting to him from 21 to 12 and eliminated $56 million in operating costs."[9] Imagine having all this activity in play when suddenly the organization takes a sharp turn with a new CEO who puts everything on hold. For us, taking control and managing our own culture in this environment meant that we could stay focused on delivering what was important to our region. In turn, the stability in our region provided positive results for the rest of the organization.

Improving Culture Improves Performance

None of our organizations are perfect; they always have room for improvement. Improvements can be made on a mass scale, such as introducing a new performance management system, or they can be made on a micro-level, such as coaching a single employee. You can change culture by implementing a large full-scale movement from the top, or you can change culture by taking ownership of your immediate influence on those working directly with you. You don't need to be the leader from on high to make a shift in your organization's culture. In fact, you could be like that pebble in the pond and start a ripple effect that spreads out across your organization.

I saw this ripple effect as our team dispersed into new roles and duties. All our team members still see themselves as the generals of their individual operations. And each general continues the challenge of culture with every new team. Sometimes, in order to win the war, you have to win a series of battles.

These battles may take place in different parts of the organization, and they may range from big battles to small skirmishes. Each part of the organization comes from a different place when you start your cultural journey. Sure, it takes a long time to move the whole army, and you may never fully advance it if your top general insists on maintaining a different direction or goal. However, the more you can influence the spheres around you, the more you can ensure the success of your troops.

And as it turned out, Headquarters did step up again and begin a more robust cultural journey for the entire company. Now Headquarters is an ally, focused on making changes in those parts of the company that need it the most. This makes our job even easier as all employees start marching in the same direction.

Don't let the fact that you're working in the trenches in the middle of your organization stop you from improving your culture. Every operation needs a strong line of defense and an offense that keeps moving forward. You can, and should be, the commander in charge of the corporate culture around you.

FUEL FOR THOUGHT

🔥 Are you leading your troops or waiting for orders from Headquarters?

🔥 What's stopping you from becoming your own general?

🔥 What can you change within your team members' culture to muster them to a common purpose?

CHAPTER SEVENTEEN

Igniting Merger Potential

Disney and Pixar, Sears and Kmart, Quaker Oats and Snapple, Cathy's Convenience and Sam's Smokes. Mergers and acquisitions, large and small, are common occurrences as companies search for ways to augment their profitability. They're also famous for all the due diligence necessary to turn a handshake into a final financial, regulatory, and legal document.

Due diligence appears in all forms. Every line item is audited, valuations are appraised, physical assets are inventoried. Binders and binders of checklists and documentation build up in the war room. Discussions go on and on, back and forth. Task forces are sent into the satellite locations where employees are questioned endlessly. Every type of document, invoice, policy manual, and client data is inspected, challenged, and verified. These times are exciting and stressful for the people of both organizations. "What's in our future if this deal goes through?"

Next come the lawyers who transcribe all the language around the exchange of money, the timing of the merger, and so on. At last, the companies reach the proverbial celebratory signing of the agreements, including an elaborate dinner with expensive wine and handshakes around the table. At this point, employees are asking, "The future is here. What does this mean for me?"

Then comes the work to physically merge the two operations. Sometimes, the two organizations continue as before, with the acquired business operating as a distinct business unit. Sometimes the new organization gets fully enveloped into the parent. Operational integration can take many forms. In some cases, management simply drops new policy manuals and organization charts on every desk and leaves people to fend for themselves to learn the new way of working. In other cases, they draw up detailed plans for every function within the merged business and guide employees through the integration process.

And yet, 70 percent of all mergers and acquisitions fail to realize the benefits envisioned when the initial seeds of the deal were planted with that first handshake. For some reason, unexpected costs and larger-than-expected drops in productivity creep into what is supposed to be a more profitable venture. By now, can you guess one of the biggest contributors to this discrepancy? That's right: *lack of cultural alignment between the two organizations*. One of the most overlooked pieces in the due-diligence process is comparing the cultures of the two organizations to identify any possible misalignment.

Mergers at Rogers Communications

Rogers Communications is no stranger to acquisitions, and during my 24 years there, I participated in a number of them. The deals went down in a variety of ways, and some transitioned more successfully than others. Many started over drinks, with Ted Rogers supposedly signing a "memorandum of understanding" on a cocktail napkin. Others became high-profile events, such as the acquisition of Maclean-Hunter, a highly public hostile takeover.

In 1994, Ted Rogers orchestrated a $3.1 billion purchase of Maclean-Hunter, then the largest takeover in Canadian history and one of the first big bets on communications convergence of media content, television, and Internet—bringing together communication delivery and media/content. Then smaller deals occurred, such as Rogers' acquisition of Cable Atlantic in Newfoundland, in which the equally charismatic leader at the time, Danny Williams, yearned to move on into Canadian politics.

In the case of the Rogers/Maclean-Hunter acquisition, the entrepreneurial, highly debt-leveraged Rogers faced the challenge of enveloping the stable, straightforward, and fiscally responsible Maclean-Hunter. In the Cable Atlantic merger, Rogers became the large Toronto-centric conglomerate swooping up the family-oriented east coasters. While Rogers was seen as a fast-paced partner compared to Maclean-Hunter, the company ultimately came across as a complicated and bureaucratic partner to the former employees of Cable Atlantic.

In all cases, no matter how Rogers's acquisition deals were originally formulated, the pattern was always the same. The companies announced that their two leaders had entered into an agreement. Months and months of due diligence followed. I recall going through boxes upon boxes of documents as we verified all assets, customer counts, and financial information.

Then, when it came time to integrate the operations of the new properties into the Rogers machine, we focused mainly on transferring customer accounts into the Rogers billing systems, linking the telecom networks, and adding the acquired employees into the various purchasing and HR systems. Everything centered on numbers: number of customer accounts, number of kilometers of cable infrastructure, number of employees to be trained. Eventually, all the financial and legal approvals would fall into place. The deals were formally signed, the celebrations began again, and a "welcome" memo came down from the "castle on high." Then, the planning of operational integration we'd been running parallel to the due diligence would start to come alive.

Exciting New Chapter, Right?

It happens all the time: a new organization is announced, some people lose their jobs, and other people move into new offices and new roles. The offices become a blend of the combined workforces. A new exciting chapter begins in the life of the expanded company. Or does it?

Let's look at another example. The culture at Skyline Cablevision, an Ottawa cable system acquired by Rogers in 1991, had been one of command and control. The executive team held information tightly, the workforce relied on union representation to communicate with management, and employees felt their work went unrecognized. The story goes that when the company president handed out bonus checks at the Christmas party, someone had to stand at his shoulder and whisper the name of the employee in his ear.

When Rogers took over Skyline Cablevision, we failed to review these cultural issues during the due-diligence process. When the acquisition became final, we moved in one day and continued to run business as usual. Except there was nothing usual about it.

By comparison, Rogers appeared much more people oriented. The leadership team was much more visible and engaged with their employees, Rogers upgraded the uniforms and tools, and people were empowered to run their own departments. During the first year of the Skyline merger, every company event featured Tina Turner's "Simply the Best" as a theme song. Employees welcomed improved benefits including better health insurance coverage and financial support for education upgrades. That is, the non-union employees welcomed them. Eventually, the unionized employees decertified from their union, a resounding vote of confidence in the new leaders and the Rogers organization.

However, with empowerment also came accountability. Under the command and control regime, managers did not have to make decisions; they simply did what they were told. While Rogers provided training on processes, policies, and systems, we failed to recognize the need for soft skills training like decision making, employee coaching, and financial acumen. We just expected these newly empowered managers to step into their newfound autonomy.

I remember meeting with the new management team when the first budgeting cycle came around. As I presented the budgeting process and spreadsheets, that "deer in the head-lights" look gradually spread across the faces of those around the boardroom table. Their expressions seemed to say, "I'm going to be accountable for *what*? You expect me to make *financial* decisions?" Without the right support mechanism in place, fear could have set in quickly. Many of the managers had skills to help the others: Denis was an expert in spreadsheets, Debbie was an expert in workforce scheduling, Catalina was the accountant and could support and direct people through the financial information. I had regular one-on-one check-in points during the two-week budgeting time frame to make sure the managers were staying on track. I didn't just walk out of that boardroom and leave them without lifejackets in the middle of the ocean.

Yes, the new management team shifted to accept the Rogers culture. Ultimately, they welcomed the move away from a command-and-control culture toward one based on recognition, trust, and empowerment. Had we understood at the outset where the cultural differences lay, we could have accomplished the shift much more quickly.

Two Different Cultures

The Maclean-Hunter merger proved to be a different animal. The sheer size of this acquisition was enormous. Maclean-Hunter had a reputation as a disciplined, profitable, steeped-in-history organization. Employees felt proud to be a part of this Canadian icon. In their minds, the upstart Rogers had forced its way into their world when it should have been the other way around. Again, we faced the challenge of merging two different cultures, but this time each culture had strong champions. And neither culture was "right" or "wrong." Both had been working effectively, and neither camp felt an impetus to change. For our Ottawa organization, the change also meant combining two cable companies from the same geographic region. As a result, duplication was everywhere. Merging the two organizations and selecting the best people from each posed another huge challenge.

Once again, the due-diligence process never assessed the two cultures. Maclean-Hunter employees had no support to understand and adjust to the Rogers entrepreneurial culture. Yet we shuffled the two groups together like two decks of cards.

Our differences manifested most clearly in our two different approaches to upgrading the networks. Maclean-Hunter was slow and steady, efficient and economic. Rogers was fast and innovative, with large amounts of equipment and many people to manage in a short period of time. The ideal was "nothing but the latest and greatest," with the implication that cost didn't matter. The Maclean-Hunter engineers were flabbergasted by the demands, confused by the approach, and committed to maintaining a cost-effective rebuild. The Rogers engineers pushed and pushed, demanding faster designs and decisions.

Employees floundered, testing the waters on how to work with each other. Eventually, people sorted it out. In the meantime, however, subcultures continued to develop. Values that some people viewed positively, such as process, struck others as negative bureaucracy. Getting things done required more and

more effort, and productivity started to suffer. Instead of stra-
tegically using the original culture of Rogers as a springboard
for the future, we'd ignored the issue of culture—and now each
organization had adopted a mish-mash of cultures.

More Merger Challenges

The Cable Atlantic merger also presented unique challenges. While the Maclean-Hunter merger had doubled the size of
Rogers' cable division, Cable Atlantic, a small cable company
in Newfoundland, would increase our base by less than 10 percent. Clearly, this was not a merger of equals. However, Cable
Atlantic was extremely profitable. And befitting the culture in
that part of the country, the company culture was highly family
oriented. Proud, accountable, and empowered, the leaders ran
their own ships. Then Rogers swooped in, centralized operations, and introduced all kinds of processes and policies necessary to run a large corporation.

For Cable Atlantic employees, everything took much longer.
Business once resolved with a conversation in the hallway now
required a report to the head office to introduce an initiative.
If the idea got support, it might take layers of approvals before
implementation could begin. And since the merged employees
were now small fish in a big pond, in many cases just getting
their voices heard was a challenge. I remember many conversations with Cable Atlantic executive Ken Marshall, trying to
explain why Rogers did things the way it did. Meanwhile, Ken
saw the profitability of his organization slide because he had to
introduce more and more support to deal with the perceived

bureaucracy. And with the head office half a country away, the family dynamics just didn't work anymore.

Valuable Lessons

To different degrees, all three of these mergers can teach leaders a valuable lesson: Cultural misalignments can sabotage merger benefits. If that happens, it takes energy and resources to turn the situation around. Time passes, opportunities fly by, and costs add up. Doing a cultural assessment of both organizations *before* a merger as part of the due-diligence process, however, will highlight areas of difference and head off problems at the pass. Then, during the integration of the two operations, leadership can implement a culture-focused change-management plan to ease employees into the new environment and quickly restore full productivity.

In hindsight, Rogers also could have introduced conversations about values and culture with the merged companies' employees during the process of bringing them on board. We could have included 360-degree values-based assessments for each member of the management team to use in developing plans to help them through the culture shift. If we'd conducted a cultural assessment as part of our planning, we would have identified the cultural areas that needed focus in our change-management strategies. In addition, we would have created a very different employee communication plan. Finally, we would have identified potential areas of concern early on—places where it looked like employees might not be able to make the shift.

In fact, the time to initiate cultural due diligence is as soon as acquisition talks begin. Leaders spend a lot of time analyzing the *benefits* of bringing two companies together. However, too often they fail to look at the effort it will take to create a seamless operation from the merger of the organizations. And the more company leaders seek to integrate the two entities, the more important it is for them to take culture into account.

In the Maclean-Hunter example, Rogers could have chosen to continue to run the two Ottawa call centers separately. In this case, doing so would have lessened the cultural impact, as each center could continue to operate as before and maintain the existing cultures for the most part. However, Rogers believed that integrating the two groups into one call center would advance efficiency. Furthermore, understanding the groups' cultural differences up front would have allowed Rogers to plan for the impact of change, including the confusion and anxiety that resulted from the decision to combine the call centers. Giving employees a framework for important company values and how to work together could have helped keep engagement levels and productivity up.

Why do 70 percent of mergers and acquisitions fail to realize their economic benefits? I believe this failure results when not enough effort goes into assessing the effect of the merger on employees and their company values. When these values misalign, employees misdirect their energy toward problems and productivity suffers. *How* the work gets done is just as important as *what* gets done, even during an acquisition.

FUEL FOR THOUGHT

🔥 Have you considered the cultural differences between your company and any potential partners?

🔥 How can you more effectively bring merged employee groups together?

🔥 What changes will you have to make to your current culture to ensure the success of a merged organization?

CHAPTER EIGHTEEN

Culture and Crisis

Ten years ago, who would've thought that General Motors and Chrysler would file for bankruptcy? The meltdown of our global financial markets was not on most people's radar screens. How many businesses survive their entire existence without ever facing a crisis?

It doesn't matter what size business or industry you're in; crisis can and will appear. It may come as a result of adversity, or it can even come as a result of success. An unexpected environmental disaster, such as a tsunami or earthquake, may trigger a crisis throughout an entire region. Or the crisis may be an individual company's financial failure. Crisis may appear overnight or be the result of the final straw that breaks the proverbial camel's back.

Those businesses with strong, positive corporate cultures are best prepared when crisis hits. In the words of Steven Thulon, a senior master sergeant of the U.S. Air Force, "Conflict builds culture, however crisis defines it." Because culture exists either by design or by default, waiting for a crisis to occur before you examine your organizational culture is like playing the lottery. You never know what numbers will come up. Moreover, crisis is hardly the time to find out your culture can't support you through the emergency.

While change has become constant in our business world, crisis, catastrophe, and chaos also crop up at more and more alarming rates. Organizational resilience is essential to weather the storms. And while financial resilience will go a long way toward pulling an organization out of crisis, it's the character of your employees that will ultimately decide which side of the challenge you come out on: success or failure. As leaders, we must prepare for the unexpected, and leaving our culture in a default status instead of shaping it into a managed status only increases our risk. For some lucky companies, the default culture will help you through the disaster. If not, the disaster will take on even larger proportions.

Brutal Storm, Brilliant Response

In January 1998, Canadians living in eastern Ontario experienced a brutal ice storm—supposedly the region's largest recorded environmental crisis. And while winters in Ottawa are known for snow and cold, the storm that blew through that January wasn't one of those gentle, fluffy snowstorms that inspire us to run outside and catch snowflakes on our tongues. It was a raging storm that blew pellets of ice sideways across the region—not for an hour but for five days! The ice settled on everything: rooftops, streets, trees, and power lines. Hour after hour, day after day, the coat of ice grew thicker and heavier until tree branches, hydro lines, and even hydro poles snapped. Homes and businesses were slammed into darkness.

When the storm finally passed and the clouds dispersed, the region resembled a war zone. Between Quebec and Ontario, the storm broke 35,000 telecommunication poles, put 5,000 hydro transformers out of commission, damaged 1,000 hydro-style pylons, and collapsed 300 steel hydro towers. Millions of people lost power and heat. Internet and television were disrupted. Communications were reduced to battery-powered radios and daily newspapers.

For those of us in the Ottawa cable business, crisis had arrived! Over 2,000 aerial cable lines had snapped, leaving thousands of homes without cable communications to the outer world. Our phone lines were jammed with customers wanting to know when their services would be up and running. For perspective, our crews normally handle approximately 1,800 broken lines a year. The storm dumped 14 months of work in our lap in two days! Crisis had arrived not only to our communities but also to our business.

While the city called in the armed forces to help restore the damaged hydro poles and lines, we knew we were on our own. Fortunately, we'd established a culture of teamwork-because we needed it more than ever. Instantaneously, we convened in the main boardroom and formed a "war room." The 10 of us around that table didn't know where to start, given the enormity of the situation. We all looked at Dennis, the technical director, wondering how he would find enough manpower to complete all the field work that lay ahead. We looked at Annette, our technical support call center director, wondering how she'd answer hundreds of phone calls with half her staff stuck in their homes trying to manage their own personal crises. Not only did we need to manage the business, we also needed to provide support to many of our employees who were without power or day care or whose family members required assistance.

What tools helped us dig our way out of the ice-storm crisis? We fell back on the values our leadership team shared: teamwork, accountability, customer focus, respect, and service. Because we deemed these values necessary for success, we'd built our organization around them. If we'd had a culture of personal gain, risk aversion, and resistance to change, it would have taken us months to restore our services. In the meantime, our customers likely would have sought out other suppliers that didn't have services dependent on direct lines to the house, and our revenues would have taken a beating. The impact to our bottom line—and ultimately to our employees—would have been disastrous. Our brand would have been damaged, jeopardizing future sales.

Instead, I was never prouder of my team than I was as we pulled through that ice-storm crisis. We sourced every available, skilled body from across the company—even crews from New Brunswick. Sales people became order managers. Team managers used their creativity and customer focus to create new processes that could meet the scale of the situation. A second team assumed accountability for supporting our affected employees. The company value of communication overarched the response of both teams.

If teamwork was the first priority, accountability was right behind. Because we'd already defined these values, we didn't have to spend time going around people or fighting with people to step up. Because these values were core to our company, they came naturally. As a result, we were able to focus our energies on responding to the crisis, not battling each other. After all, our energies were stretched thin to begin with, and we just didn't have the capacity to take on new internal crises during an external one. As Henry Kissinger once said, "There cannot be a crisis today; my schedule is already full."

Not Always Smooth at Zappos

Even the great Zappos online shoe and clothing company faced a crisis in its early years. From 2001 to 2002, it suffered from a lack of funding that often pushed it to the brink before it found just enough cash to carry it forward for another quarter. Already, the new start-up company faced a recession, the dot.com crash, and 9/11. Venture funding was just as difficult to find then as it is today after the global market crash. It was inevitable that Zappos would go into survival mode and lay off employees. Yet, the company did survive and grew its gross revenues from $8.6 million in 2001 to $32 million in 2002!

For the Zappos folks, laying off employees felt like a downward spiral toward closing the company. Crisis had arrived at the front door. So how did the company turn things around and end up with $32 million in gross sales that year? CEO Tony Hsieh found that the people laid off were the "underperformers and non-believers." Everyone left behind felt so passionate about Zappos that overall productivity didn't decrease. That remaining core team all shared values allowing them to focus on the right priorities of the day. They even revamped their distribution model, a bold move in the midst of a financial squeeze. Tony didn't know how Fred, the vice president of merchandising, would convince enough other brands to join them in this new distribution model in such a short timeframe. Fred didn't know how Tony would find the money to bring in-house all the company's inventory warehousing and shipping. But they trusted each other.

Waiting for a crisis to find out about your culture is its own crisis waiting to happen. And while an external crisis can take you out of business, fielding an internal people crisis at the same time can leave you feeling crushed under the weight of the world. When other companies around you face a similar crisis, your chances of survival are far better if you only have to deal with the primary crisis than the chances of companies that face multiple waves of crises.

Are you willing to gamble your organization's success in crisis? What are your competitors doing to be ready? Having the right culture during the best of times is a competitive advantage; imagine the advantage it gives you during a time of crisis.

Surviving crisis is also incredibly empowering. For instance, surviving the ice storm in Ottawa gave me the confidence and motivation to face any other challenges coming my way. Going forward, Rogers set bigger objectives and goals for our business plans than we'd ever considered before. A new product launch? No problem! We knew our core values and culture had been on target before the crisis because they held up during the crisis.

And what about Zappos? The company has gone on to generate over $1 billion in gross sales and were ranked at 23 on Fortune's 2009 list of the 100 Best Companies to work for—its first appearance on that list. The values of passion, creativity, and customer service its people displayed during times of crisis in the early years helped propel the company forward to great success today.

Resilient organizations get their strength from their people. Surviving a crisis depends on a strong, cohesive team that's also knowledgeable, adaptable, and innovative. Organizations that consciously manage their culture are closer to understanding what it takes to make sure their organizations can pull through catastrophe.

Many organizations go through risk assessments; some even go one further and build contingency plans. However, successful implementation of these efforts falls to the people in the organization. Again, the best plans in a binder are useless if employees don't have the capacity to execute them. In a crisis, you won't have time to train people to work together, and you may not have the luxury of calling up reinforcements who can step in immediately. When those reinforcements do arrive, will your processes scale up to meet the demands of the situation? When the armed forces arrived to help city utility workers during the ice-storm crisis, they brought their hard-wired skill with logistics and planning, as well as the training to work on large-scale operations. City employees needed to adapt quickly to a new leadership style as they worked together with the armed forces to restore electricity, light, heat, and communications.

"Anyone can steer a ship when the sea is calm," said Pubili-us Syrus. It's up to you as a leader to make sure that not only can you guide your ship on a calm sea, but you also prepare your crew for all types of adventures.

When the next storm blows in, I know I'd rather have a boat full of highly trained Olympic-caliber rowers than a ship full of misfit pirates.

FUEL FOR THOUGHT

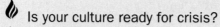 Is your culture ready for crisis?

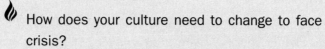 How does your culture need to change to face crisis?

What part of your organization needs the most focus today to prepare for tomorrow's crisis?

CHAPTER NINETEEN

Igniting the Potential of the Rings

"The most important thing in the Olympic Games is not winning but taking part; the essential thing in life is not conquering but fighting well."
—**Pierre de Coubertin**,
founder of the modern Olympic Games

Make no mistake; the Olympic Games are big business, occurring every two years and ranging in budget from $1 billion to $7 billion, with the exception of Greece's Athens event in 2004 at $15 billion. In addition to the direct costs of putting on this international event, each game also has ancillary costs and profits. But despite the reports about cost and budget overruns that lead up to each game, at the end of the day, the Olympics draw almost 4 billion viewers worldwide. That's four times the number of members on Facebook!

What is it about the values of the Olympic Games that transcends business to bring people together in such a meaningful way? Sure, governments invest in the business of the games with sports programs that provide the best possible coaching, equipment, and opportunity to collect medals. But when10,000 athletes from more than 200 National Athletic Associations stand together peacefully under the symbol of the Olympic rings, that's the image we remember. Despite the differences between our nations in economic and governmental policies, sport gives us common ground.

Does your business serve a higher calling or does it exist only to earn profits for the owners or shareholders? Most companies exist to provide a service to a particular market. Services run the spectrum of Maslow's hierarchy of needs, which we saw in Chapter 10. We feed, clothe, and house our communities, and also provide policing, fire protection, and personal security. We provide health care and education as well as jobs and the opportunity to gain financial security. We develop entertainment centers, community centers, religious centers, and sports centers where families can grow and interact with each other. We offer a governmental system in which individuals can actively participate in the collective achievement of making our neighborhoods better. Plus, we make charitable outlets available where we can donate dollars or personal time to better serve those less fortunate.

Providing services to our customers, jobs to our employees, and returns to our shareholders are the most basic and fundamental reasons that businesses exist. Yet we all strive to improve our businesses. We innovate to create new products and procedures, and in the process, we move our civilization forward. And increasingly, today's younger generations are calling businesses to demonstrate corporate social responsibility.

When the businesses of a nation thrive and grow, so does the country in general. So what conditions do our nations require to ensure economic and social wealth as we hope our businesses do? If the right corporate values can help companies become more effective in providing services beyond sustaining the bottom line, then can't the same be true for nations?

What national values need to be in place to ensure our nations are effective and grow to meet the demands of their people and the ever-changing climates that exist in our global world? In the same way we determine limiting values that can be detrimental to the success of a company, can we determine what national values limit the success of our nations?

Consider what happened in Australia, starting with a small group of friends—all from the nonprofit sector—discussing their workplace challenges in a pub.[10] As often happens in such discussions, common challenges emerged, and the group traded different perspectives and insights. Over time, leaders from other sectors joined the growing group. As true leaders, these people decided to push beyond the status quo to establish a shared vision. As a result, in August 2009, they established Emerging Leaders for Social Change (ELSC).

Today, ELSC's membership consists of emerging leaders from social, government, and private sectors. The Centre for Social Impact, a collaboration of business schools from the four Australian Universities, also supports the ELSC with important academic insights.

One of the key initiatives established by the ELSC is called "The Big Conversation":

There has been an explosion of conversations about what the global economic crisis
means for all of us, what the future holds and
what needs to change. The government is asking us to tell them what is important to us. We
need to make these important conversations
bigger and **louder**. We need to talk about **our
values**, because this is where our decisions and
our actions come from. What values best reflect
how our society should operate? What values
does our society want to see in the future? We
want to know what Australians think. We want
to start a conversation. A Big Conversation! [11]

In late 2009, the Big Conversation engaged more than
2,000 Australians in a National Values Assessment. The overall
results portray a community that personally values relationships
and self-development, with a strong sense of unity. The top 10
personal values cited were: family, honesty, caring, humor/fun,
friendship, respect, compassion, independence, responsibility,
and trust. By comparison, with regard to the current culture
of Australia, the results reflected the global financial crisis. The
top 10 current values of the nation were: bureaucracy, crime/
violence, blame, wasted resources, materialism, corruption, un-
certainty about the future, short-term focus, freedom of speech,
and economic growth. And finally, the Australians surveyed defined the culture that they would *like* to see in their nation:
caring for the elderly, affordable housing, accountability, caring

for the disadvantaged, concern for future generations, effective healthcare, employment opportunities, community pride, governmental effectiveness, and dependable public services.

Following the survey, the ELSC shared the results in a number of forums and summits. They defined three areas of focus,[12] each with its own dedicated task force:

- Create greater public awareness around the need to define a new Australian Dream.

- Influence greater values-based decision making in a broad range of decision makers in Australia by promoting conversations and values-based tools.

- Influence the inclusion of an annual values survey, alongside the Well Being Index, for inclusion in the national measures of health of the country.

These leaders in Australia have taken the business principle of a values-driven organization and applied it at the national level. Australia is now striving to redefine itself and put itself in a position of global competitiveness by reducing the costs and wasted energy associated with the limiting values of bureaucracy, blame, and wasted resources. And this work has not been dumped on the government alone; the initiative is a call to all sectors to embrace the people's desire to move away from these limiting attributes.

For Iceland, the journey has not been so smooth. An August 2008 National Values Assessment predicted the country's declaration of bankruptcy, which came to pass that October. At the time, those surveyed described the current culture as one of materialism, short-term focus, corruption, elitism, wasted resources, gender discrimination, and blame.

Bjarni Jonsson has been a passionate advocate for change in Iceland ever since he first started studying Icelandic culture in 2005. Following the economic collapse, Jonsson made a formal proposal to the prime minister to discuss the rebirth of Iceland, based on his research on values. While interested, the prime minister was also overwhelmed with the current state of the nation, and in fact, the sitting government failed and dissolved in January 2009. After several other failed attempts to get people engaged, a group formed in mid-2009 that included a government minister, a world-renowned pop artist, a well-known Icelandic entrepreneur, a consultant, a chairman of a specialized asset-management company, a university associate professor, an actress and theater director, and a film director. As Jonsson noted, "The group covered the spectrum from outspoken social activists to business people, with opinion ranging about 180°."[13] They named themselves "The Anthill" based on the analogy that a whole anthill can be moved away from a threatening situation, such as an overflowing river, by the ants themselves.

In November 2009, the group hosted a National Assembly consisting of 1,200 randomly selected citizens and 300 leaders from NGOs, government, parliament, and institutions. Immediately after the dissolution, two other sitting parties—the Social Democrats and the Left Greens—formed a coalition government. The leader of the Social Democrats became the new prime minister and remained in power until May 2013. At the end of the summit, nine themes emerged, each with its own vision statement. In addition, the desired values most often cited were honestly/integrity, equality, respect, and justice. In 2010, a second National Assembly resulted in a mandate to generate principles for a new national constitution. On July 29, 2011, The Anthill submitted a bill on the new constitution to the government, which was unanimously approved. Since that time, the Icelandic parliament has engaged in two years of endless debate, the opposition parties refusing to support the proposed changes. With a new election in the works, the constitution rests in limbo.

Despite these efforts, a 2010 reassessment by the Barrett Values Centre[14] revealed that the current culture of Iceland may be falling into greater disrepair. Unemployment, concern for future generations, conflict/aggression, and poverty emerged as additional limiting values from the first survey.

National values are shaped by the communities within a geographic border. If our personal values develop based on each of our experiences and beliefs over a lifetime, imagine how our community's values are also shaped by events over time. Much as external events shape the values of different generations, so do they shape geographic values. And in some cases, geographic values have also been shaped by centuries of tradition.

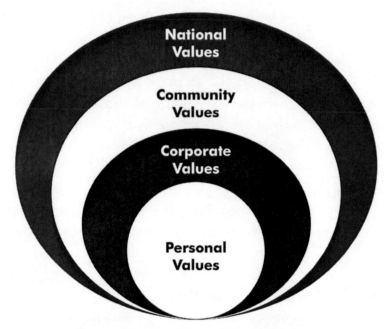

Figure 19.1 The Ripple Effect of Values

Reducing limiting values within our nations will improve our success, whether that means attracting and retaining the best talent within our national businesses, or resilience and competitiveness on the global market. Our success also depends on providing the basics to our citizens, such as housing, elderly care, and employment opportunities. Creating a strong national culture requires effort from all levels—from the grassroots as well as from our governments. Australia is now defining a new national dream in this manner. In other countries, the state of the national culture has never been adequately assessed.

Rogers Communication's CEO Ted Rogers, a proud Canadian, never forgot his Canadian roots. His vision was to build the largest national telecommunications company serving Canadians from coast to coast. It's no accident that the corporate colors at Rogers are red and white, the colors of the Canadian flag. Many of the company's innovative new products are launched on Canada Day, July 1. Rogers incorporated his personal value of service to nation in a way that never let his employees forget our company's national obligation.

Each and every one of us has the ability to influence our national cultures because ultimately, individuals create national cultures. It's up to us to stay engaged, not become complacent. Complacency is akin to condoning limiting values. To improve our national cultures, we must improve our own corporate cultures as well as be active guardians of governmental actions and policies that have an impact on those cultures. We need to stay informed on shifts in our national culture to prevent the slippery slope of worsening conditions like Iceland's, and instead ensure that we have avenues to participate in big conversations like Australia's.

In the same manner, each of us has the ability to influence the cultures of other nations. In 1998, as a result of his first-grade project, young Ryan Hreljac decided to raise $70 to pay for a water well in Africa. For four months, he did extra chores to raise this money—but then he found out it would actually take $2,000 to build a well. Undeterred, he went on to raise the money and at the age of seven funded his first well. Three years later, at the ripe age of 10, he created the Ryan's Well Foundation, which to date has helped build more than 724 water projects serving more than 750,000 Africans.

At the other end of the spectrum, the Bill and Melinda Gates Foundation started with the support of great wealth that had been amassed by Bill Gates through his Microsoft organization. The foundation's purpose reads, "Rather than look at the challenges that people face by region we identify challenges that can be tackled on a global level. We work with partners that can help to affect change globally, and then scale solutions to a local level." The Gates Foundation provided more than $3 billion in grants in 2011.

To change the world, do we need to be a Ryan or a Bill? Do we need to lead a campaign on the scale of Australia's Big Conversation to create a better national culture? Absolutely not; these are heady challenges. However, can we align our values to make our world substantially better than it is today? Definitely! If the athletes of hundreds of nations can stand together peacefully under the values of the Olympic Games, then better awareness and implementation of our personal values can certainly improve our communities and businesses—and indeed influence entire nations.

FUEL FOR THOUGHT

🔥 Where will you make changes in your corporate culture to help influence the values of your community?

🔥 How can your business contribute to a shift toward a stronger national culture?

🔥 How will you show up in the Big Conversation?

Conclusion

L ife is too short to be miserable, whether it's at home or at the office. I don't believe we are brought into this world to be miserable. And yet over time, many of us become passive passengers on this planet Earth. In order to be more engaged in the things that matter to us, understanding our personal values is critical. Aligning those values to the circumstances that are going on in our lives brings about energy, laughter, and a sense of wellbeing.

And to the degree that we all want more of these benefits in our lives, creating them at the office is just as important as creating them in our personal lives. Aligning our personal values with our organization's values, while they're never perfectly aligned, makes us welcome the idea of going to work. We no longer need to pull the covers over our heads and try to deny the alarm clock every morning. We can wake up knowing that the day ahead is not about work; it's about contribution, purpose, and potential.

As leaders, while we owe our shareholders and owners a profitable bottom line, we also owe our employees the best possible workplaces. Pushing for the right culture for today and evolving it as we grow into tomorrow is an obligation I believe we should all own. It doesn't matter where we are in the organization; we can make an impact on culture. If collectively we can build better organizations and encourage and be energized employees, then collectively we can have an influence on our communities. It's the pebble in the pond phenomenon. One pebble tossed in the water can create ripples all across the pond.

That's why I'm passionate about connecting culture to process, people, and strategy and why I'm convinced it's so key. This connection and the power of this partnership fuels results. We can focus on just the financials, or we can create better financials by creating better cultures. To create better cultures, we need to do that analysis and take the sludge out of our organizational fuel. By addressing the limiting values, developing a blueprint for action, and staying committed to the journey, we can design powerful and positive places to work.

Every era has its challenges. In this era of ever-growing globalization, our challenges are becoming more and more connected. The financial crisis of a single company (think Enron), the failure within a broad industry (think banking, the dot-com bust), or the bankruptcy of a nation (Iceland) affects a broader audience than ever before. We need strong organizations, strong communities, and strong nations. Strength comes from a culture of positive values tied to a common purpose. The stronger the culture, the higher the purpose.

As leaders, it's our behaviors and beliefs that ultimately define our values and the culture of our organizations. Therefore, it's up to us to accept the challenge, embrace the tools and process of IGNITE, and begin our journey to full potential today!

Fuel for Thought Summary

1. Culture's Influence on Corporate Results
    - Are you letting culture *eat* your strategy?
    - Has your company performance been successful in spite of setbacks?
    - How will you embrace the cultural capital frontier and deal yourself the best possible hand?
2. How Leaders Fuel Culture
    - What are you as leaders in your organization doing to contribute to your corporate culture?
    - How much of your corporate culture is a direct result of the personal values of your leadership team?
    - How honest are you being about your role in the creation of your division's culture?
3. How Employees Fuel Culture
    - Do you know what values are important to your employees?
    - Have you measured the degree of your employees' personal alignment to your ideal corporate culture?
    - If you knew this, what ingredients could you add to foster high performance in that unit?
4. The Building Blocks of Culture
    - Are you crystal clear about your personal values?
    - If you've taken on too much, what could you say no to?
    - How aligned is your work to your personal values?

5. Evolving Culture
   - How will you celebrate and maintain your momentum for lasting culture change—and not simply create the next fad in your company?
   - What tools do you need to pack as you continue your journey?
   - Where will you find additional support and strength to lead your company through ongoing changes in the business world around you?
6. Poor Culture, Poor Company
   - Do you know if your current culture contains any limiting or negative values?
   - How could those limiting values be affecting the performance of your organization, creating sludge in your corporate fuel?
   - What are the costs of your culture's limiting values?
7. Fueling Your Brand
   - Does your culture support your brand?
   - What questions do you need to ask your marketing and executive teams to make sure your culture and brand align with each other?
   - How authentic is your brand?
8. The IGNITE process
   - Are you ready to move your organization to the launch pad?
   - How can adopting the IGNITE process benefit your company?
   - What resources will you need to help you through the IGNITE process?

9. I is for Inquire
   - What tools in your life have made things considerably easier?
   - Are you ready to embrace and champion a tool to inquire into your organization's culture?
   - What demographic inquiries will best serve your organization?
10. G is for Gather
   - Are you willing to invest time and effort in gathering research?
   - What resources will you need to help you gather all the feedback?
   - How open will you be to listen your employees' stories?
11. N is for Name
   - What ingredients do you need to add to your cultural recipe to maximize the fuel?
   - What interim steps might you need to take toward your optimum culture?
   - What criteria will you use to select your top three to five core values?
12. I is for Imbed
   - What filters will you use to prioritize all the ideas and initiatives that can shift your culture?
   - How committed is your leadership team to its part of the blueprint?
   - How will you keep your blueprint alive as your organization evolves?

13. T is for Track, E is for Evaluate
    - How can you ensure the progress of your cultural journey through measurement?
    - How will you give your cultural journey the priority it needs when it comes to reporting organizational results?
    - Have you set a target for evaluating the success of your blueprint?
14. "Why Don't They Do What I Say?"
    - Do you have a clear understanding of change management?
    - What do you need to do to formalize change management within your organization?
    - Where can you best use change management to ensure the success of your culture change?
15. Generational Culture
    - Do you know the generational makeup of your organization?
    - What impact does this have on the culture of your organization?
    - What shifts in your organizational culture do you need to consider now in order to hire the best talent from Generation Y?
16. Culture from the Management Trenches
    - Are you leading your troops or waiting for orders from Headquarters?
    - What's stopping you from being your own general?
    - What can you change within your team members' culture to muster them to a common purpose?

17. Igniting Merger Potential
    - Have you considered the cultural differences between your company and any potential partners?
    - How can you more effectively bring merged employee groups together?
    - What changes will you have to make to your current culture to ensure the success of a merged organization?
18. Culture and Crisis
    - Is your culture ready for crisis?
    - How does your culture need to change to face crisis?
    - What part of your organization needs the most focus today to prepare for tomorrow's crisis?
19. Igniting the Potential of the Rings
    - Where will you make changes in your corporate culture to help influence the values of your community?
    - How can your business contribute to a shift toward a stronger national culture?
    - How will you show up in the Big Conversation?

Acknowledgments

I would like to express my sincere appreciation to the many people who worked with me to bring this book to life. It started with Patti Pokorchak and Les Kletke at the CAPS Boot Camp. We followed that weekend with the creation of our very own Book Club. This kick-off to the book-writing process created by the two of you, was just the catalyst I needed. To you and all the other Book Club support members – Michelle Ray, Sylvia Plester-Silk, Jennifer Spear, and Janet Rouss – your encouragement, unique perspectives and advice were priceless. You stuck with me not just for a weekend, but over a series of months, and I just can't express enough gratitude for your commitment to my cause. And who knew I would not only become an author but also the Queen of the Matrix?

I would like to thank all my business colleagues who allowed me to interview them, answered endless questions and reminded me of so many experiences we have shared along the way. A very special thanks to my Rogers teams in Ottawa and Toronto for coming with me on the journey and demonstrating the power of a positive culture. Together, we grew the potential of our people and our business, and I'm so proud of all of you. At the end of the day, you are the people who inspired me to bring *Ignite Your Culture!* to life for other leaders.

I absolutely must acknowledge Richard Barrett and Phil

Clothier at the Barrett Values Centre. Your mission to build a worldwide network of change agents committed to cultural transformation is so important. I am proud to be a part of your group and I thank you for all your generous support. Ultimately it is you who inspired me to be an activist in the field of organizational culture. I am very appreciative of your particular support toward this piece of written work.

Bringing a book to life requires research, inspiration, and passion in addition to writing. However, these items only address the raw content. Massaging the thousands of words on the endless pages into a powerful finished product requires yet another team. To my editor, Barbara McNichol, many thanks for providing the power to my pen! I will always be indebted to you for bringing out the true essence of my many messages. I must also acknowledge my father, Bill Weeks, for all his editing efforts, especially since a lot of it was done between his golf games in Florida.

Next up is Janet Spencer King. You came into my life just when frustration about publishing this book was threatening to cancel the whole adventure. Your skill and expertise guided me through the ever-changing world of book printing and distribution. You also guided me through the many details required to mould a manuscript into a physical book.

Getting out the messages in this book has been a burning need for some time now. I know my family will be glad they won't have to hear me say "I have to work on my book" again any time soon. However, their ongoing belief in me, their encouragement, and their willingness to share the time with this book have sustained me. To Deane, Bob, Diane, Geoff, Conor and Amanda - thanks for your patience and understanding.

I owe a mountain of gratitude to my husband, Dennis. If I could ever pick the best partner to journey with during this arduous effort, he would be at the top of the list. From honorary Book Club member reading through everyone's chapters, to patting my hair in place when I pulled at it during my most frustrating moments; Dennis you have always, always been there as my advisor, coach, and best friend. Making space in our relationship to allow me to write this book means so much to me. I love you.

About the Author

Carol Ring is the CEO and founder of The Culture Connection, offering the "Ignite Your Culture" program that helps leaders energize their organization's values to fuel bottom-line results. Through speaking engagements, workshops and writing, Carol teaches corporate leaders how to develop a strong, vibrant company culture that is vision-guided and values-driven.

Previously, Carol worked in corporate Canada for more than 25 years. Starting as a junior accountant she eventually rose to the highest levels of corporate leadership and was voted one of Canada's most powerful women. With a last name like Ring, it's not surprising that Carol spent several decades working in the telecommunications industry. At Rogers Communications, she moved from the financial area into operations, overseeing several cable divisions including Rogers's largest one in the Greater Toronto Area. As the regional president for the GTA, she was responsible for one of the top 15 telecommunications markets in North America and its billion-dollar portfolio.

Throughout her career, Carol has filled pivotal roles in innovative product launches, acquisitions, and corporate restructuring. She has seen first-hand both the good and the bad about corporate cultures' impact on bottom-line results. Today, as a certified Cultural Transformation Tool consultant of the Barrett Values Centre, she is a passionate supporter of its mission to build a worldwide network of change agents committed to cultural transformation.

Carol has been recognized by her peers and received numerous honors. She was awarded the Fellow of the Society of Management Accountants, a prestigious national designation awarded to Certified Management Accountants for their excellence in management accounting, commitment to CMA Canada, and demonstrated civic mindedness. In 2008, Carol was recognized by the Women's Executive Network as one of Canada's Top 100 Most Powerful Women. In 2011, Canadian Women in Communications announced Carol as its Woman of the Year.

In addition to her work in the corporate world, Carol is actively involved in the community. She is a past president of the board of governors for Certified Management Accountants of Ontario, and served on the National Board of CMA Canada. Additionally, she is a past chair of the Greater Ottawa Chamber of Commerce and served on the boards of the Royal Ottawa Health Care Group, Canadian Women in Communications, and the Merry-Go-Round Children's Foundation. Carol has served on both the Toronto and Ottawa boards of the Canadian Association of Professional Speakers.

"*Ignite Your Culture: 6 Steps to Fuel Your People, Profits, and Potential*" is Carol's second book. She was the co-author of "*Awakening the Workplace: Volume 2*," and has published a number of articles including Integrated Life, Technology Overload, and Boomerang Think.

Carol currently resides in Ottawa, Ontario with her husband Dennis.

Carol invites you to email her at carol@carolring.ca and to visit her website at www.carolring.ca

Endnotes

Chapter 4

[1] Edward Hallowell, "Overloaded Circuits: Why Smart People Underperform." *Harvard Business Review*, January 2005, http://www.integrity-plus.com/eStore/WP/overload%20circuitsR0501Ef2.pdf

Chapter 7

[2] Greenpeace BP logo contest:
"BP claim that they are 'beyond petroleum.' But this is a company that is up to its neck in the dirtiest oil going—poised to invest in the Canadian tar sands, and causing environmental catastrophe through deep-water drilling. Their nice green logo doesn't really seem to fit them too well, so we ran a competition to find a logo that we could use to rebrand BP. The results are displayed here." Greenpeace UK flickr stream, accessed July 31, 2013, http://www.greenpeace.org/usa/en/news-and-blogs/news/gulf-oil-spill/bp-logo/ and http://rebrandbp.greenpeace.org.uk/

[3] BP rigger quote about cutting corners:
Mike Williams, interview by Scott Pelley, *60 Minutes*, CBS, May 16, 2010. http://www.cbsnews.com/video/watch/?id=6490509n

Chapter 9

[4] Richard Barrett, *Liberating the Corporate Soul: Building a Visionary Organisation*, Butterworth-Heinemann, Boston, 1998.

Chapter 12

[5] Jim Collins, *Good to Great: Why Some Companies Make the Leap… and Others Don't*, HarperBusiness, New York, NY, 2001.

Chapter 14

[6] John F. Kennedy, "Special Message to Congress on Urgent National Needs," Excerpt of Section IX: Space [speech before a joint session of Congress, May 25, 1961] http://www.nasa.gov/pdf/59595main_jfk.speech.pdf

[7] ADKAR model:
© Prosci. All rights reserved. ADKAR and ADKAR terms are registered trademarks of Prosci, Inc. Used with permission.

Chapter 15

[8] © Cheryl Cran. www.cherylcran.com author, *101 Ways to Make Generations X, Y and Zoomers Happy at Work* Used with permission

Chapter 16

[9] Caroline Van Hasselt, *High Wire Act: Ted Rogers and the Empire That Debt Built*, John Wiley & Sons, November 2007.

Chapter 19

[10] Australian friends' discussion source:
http://www.elsc.com.au/index.php?option=com_content&view=article&id=92&Itemid=148

[11] Lisa Doig and Karen Muller, "Creating a New Paradigm of Unstoppable Positive Social Change," *Al Practioner* Volume 12, Number 2, May 2011 http://www.corpevolution.com/assets/Uploads/Al-Practioner-Case-History-L-Doig-and-K-Muller-May-2011-Issue.pdf

[12] "Australian Unity Wellbeing Index," Australian Centre on Quality of Life at Deakin University, Australian Unity website, accessed July 31, 2013, http://www.australianunity.com.au/about-us/wellbeing/auwbi

[13] Bjarni S. Jonsson, "Notes from the Field: Iceland National Assembly," *Integral Leadership Review*, Vol. X, No. 1, January 2010 http://www.archive-ilr.com/archives-2010/2010-01/2010-01-notes-jonsson.php

[14] "National Values Assessment Iceland," Barrett Values Centre, September 2010, http://www.valuescentre.com/uploads/2010-11-04/Iceland%20National%20Values%20%20Assessment%20-%20 2010%20-%20Full%20Report%20and%20Diagrams.pdf